Multi-Threaded Programming in C++

Springer

London
Berlin
Heidelberg
New York
Barcelona
Hong Kong
Milan
Paris
Santa Clara
Singapore
Tokyo

Mark Walmsley

Multi-Threaded Programming in C++

Springer

Mark Walmsley, PhD, BSc
greengrass@btinternet.com

ISBN 1-85233-146-1 Springer-Verlag London Berlin Heidelberg

British Library Cataloguing in Publication Data
Walmsley, Mark
    Multi-threaded programming in C++
    1.C++ (computer program language)
    I.Title
    005.1'33
    ISBN 1852331461

Library of Congress Cataloging-in-Publication Data
Walmsley, Mark, 1964-
    Multi-threaded programming in C++ / Mark Walmsley.
        p.   cm.
    ISBN 1-85233-146-1 (alk. paper)
    1. C++ (Computer program language) 2. Threads (Computer programs)
    I. Title.
    QA76.73.C153W3148 1999
    005.13'3--dc21   99-40885

Typesetting: Camera-ready by author
Printed and bound by the Athenæum Press Ltd., Gateshead, Tyne & Wear
34/3830-543210 Printed on acid-free paper SPIN 10710827

Contents

Preface

This is a book about multi-threaded programming — it could well be subtitled 'How to write computer programs that do lots of different things all at once'. A multi-threaded application contains many separate threads of execution all running concurrently and each assigned to its own particular task — the individual tasks are typically simple but the combination can be very powerful. Multi-threading therefore engenders a 'divide-and-conquer' strategy which allows complex monoliths to be broken up into more manageable chunks. Indeed multi-threading is perhaps the most exciting addition to the software engineer's toolkit since the advent of object-oriented programming, another topic about which this book has a lot to say. Multi-threading and object orientation are wonderful companions — C++ allows the basic building blocks for multi-threaded programming to be neatly packaged as objects whilst multi-threading techniques can be applied to transform objects from passive repositories of functionality into active entities that perform their own internal processing independently of external code. A general background in computing is assumed as well as familiarity with the C language and a basic knowledge of C++ would also be helpful — the more useful facets of the C++ language are introduced on a 'need-to-know' basis but for a fuller exposition than is possible here the reader is advised to rush out and buy the book *'Programming in C++'* (ISBN 0 85934 435 5). The availability of a Windows or UNIX development environment (or both) would also be valuable — numerous coding examples in C++ are presented throughout the text and the book is primarily intended to accompany a practical course on multi-threaded programming that is geared towards one of these two operating systems. Nonetheless, *'Multi-Threaded Programming in C++'* should also prove to be a jolly good read for any arm-chair programmers who are interested in the subject. The three main topics of discussion are as follows:

— threads and synchronization primitives (chapters 1 to 4)
— other common multi-threading techniques (chapters 5 to 7)
— complications of more sophisticated designs (chapters 8 to 10)

Chapter 1 — An introduction to multi-threaded programming in C++.

Chapter 2 — The life-cycle of a thread and the environment within which it exists.

Chapter 3 — The 'mutex' synchronization primitive used to arbitrate amongst a number of competing threads.

Chapter 4 — The 'event' synchronization primitive used to coordinate the activities of a collection of cooperating threads.

Chapter 5 — Fundamental synchronization patterns and inter-thread communication based on 'semaphores'.

Chapter 6 — Using internal threads to activate C++ objects.

Chapter 7 — Thread-specific storage and one-time initialization.

Chapter 8 — The problem of deadlock and techniques for avoiding it.

Chapter 9 — The difficulties involved in handling multiple events.

Chapter 10 — Designing a multi-threaded distributed database application.

The book is written in pyramidal style with code from earlier chapters being re-used in later ones and so the reader is advised to follow a 'cover-to-cover' route. But enough of preliminaries — every great journey begins with the first step ...

MW
August 1999

1. Introduction

A high proportion of software currently written in C/C++ still uses a single stream of instructions ('thread') to perform its processing. However, many real-time applications (such as on-line databases or embedded process control) can benefit from the provision of multiple threads to naturally accommodate the inherent concurrency of the system. In some programming languages (Ada for example) the necessary multi-tasking facilities are built-in, but in C++ they are instead provided through a collection of multi-threading functions supported by the operating system. This chapter introduces the fundamental concepts of multi-threaded programming in C++ and covers the following key topics:

— single-threaded and multi-threaded programming
— thread synchronization primitives
— objects and classes in C++
— multi-threading under UNIX and Windows

The discussion of C++ programming is principally intended to acquaint C programmers with the notion of C++ classes — for a fuller introduction to the C++ language the reader should consult a dedicated text.

1.1 Single Threaded Programming

A traditional computer program typically comprises a list of program statements which are executed one after the other — the flow of control is basically from top to bottom with **while** or **for** loops and **if-then-else** branches providing the necessary structure. The sequence of operations that the computer performs when it runs the program constitute a single 'thread' of execution. In C/C++ this thread is defined within the main() function and any subroutines which the main() function may invoke. Whenever the user runs the program, the operating system calls the main() function and passes in any command line parameters supplied by the user. The program's one and only thread is thus activated and it then remains alive throughout the program providing all the processing required. Eventually the main() function hands control back to the operating system by returning an exit code — this action terminates the thread.

If a single-threaded program wishes to perform several different tasks simultaneously then it must implement the desired concurrency for itself.

The essential mechanism is illustrated in the following figure:

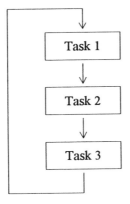

The thread actually executes the tasks sequentially but it does not fully complete one task before proceeding to the next. Instead the thread partially completes a particular task and then saves enough information about the current state of the task so that it can be resumed on the next iteration through the loop. The task switching must occur sufficiently regularly that all the tasks appear to be running together. In particular, a task must not 'block' whilst it waits for some event to occur because this will prevent all the other tasks from continuing too — a typical solution in such a situation is to periodically 'poll' for the event although this can be an inefficient option. For example, a task might block whilst awaiting user input unless it resorts to polling the state of keyboard and mouse at regular intervals.

1.2 Multi-Threaded Programming

The technique for simultaneous execution of several tasks described in the previous section has traditionally been applied to multi-tasking operating systems such as UNIX. In this case each task is associated with an independently executing 'process' and the operating system is responsible for scheduling the switches from one task to another. If several processes need to interact they can call upon various operating system services (such as signals, pipes and shared memory) that permit inter-process communication (IPC) — another possibility is simply for the processes to read and write common files in the file system.

Multi-threaded programming offers an alternative to multi-process programming that is typically less demanding of system resources — here the collection of interacting tasks are implemented as multiple threads within a single process. The programmer can regard the individual threads as running concurrently and need not implement task switching explicitly — instead this is handled by the operating system (or thread library) in a manner similar to that for task switching between processes.

The following figure illustrates the operation of a multi-threaded program as viewed by the programmer:

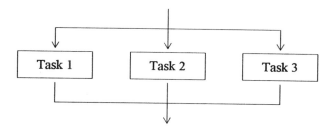

One of the threads within a process is known as the 'primary thread' and corresponds to the lone thread in a single-threaded program — it is activated when the operating system invokes the `main()` function. The primary thread is responsible for creating additional 'secondary' threads as required by the program. Each of the secondary threads executes its own 'thread function' which is analogous to the `main()` function of the primary thread — the thread functions can be passed initialization parameters and they will eventually return an exit code when the associated thread terminates. All the threads within the process share the memory space allocated to that process and so the threads can communicate directly through ordinary program variables. Chapter 2 discusses the fundamental concepts of multi-threaded programming covered here in much more detail.

1.3 Thread Synchronization

The set of threads belonging to a process all share the same resources — for example, several threads may invoke the same function to process the same piece of data. To avoid conflicts between multiple threads in such situations, some sort of synchronization mechanism is necessary. There are two basic synchronization elements:

1. mutex
2. event

A 'mutex' is used to provide mutually exclusive access to a shared resource. The resource is assigned a mutex to protect it and before a thread is allowed to manipulate the resource it must acquire the mutex — no other thread can touch the resource whilst the mutex is held. Eventually the thread using the resource will finish with it and the associated mutex will be released so that the other threads can compete to acquire it. Chapter 3 deals with the basics of handling a mutex whilst chapter 8 introduces the complications that are encountered when several resources (each requiring a mutex to protect it) are involved — a common problem that arises occurs when two threads 'deadlock' whilst each trying to acquire a resource already held by the other.

An 'event' allows one thread to signal to another thread that something has happened. Whereas a mutex arbitrates amongst a number of competing threads, an event permits several threads to coordinate their activities. For example, if one thread acts as a 'producer' of some commodity (i.e. data in a buffer) whilst another is the 'consumer' of that commodity, then the two threads can use an event to synchronize their processing. The consumer thread waits for the event to occur whilst the producer thread signals the event whenever it is ready. An important point to note is that an event contains a kind of built-in memory so that if one thread signals before another starts to wait, then the signal is not lost. Chapter 4 covers the essentials of thread synchronization using events and describes the 'producer-consumer' example in more detail. Chapter 9 extends the discussion to situations where it is necessary to simultaneously wait for several events that may occur in some unpredictable order — a common example involves events that indicate the completion of input-output (I/O) requests made to the operating system.

An event provides a binary signal ('on' or 'off') from one thread to another. A 'semaphore' is a useful generalization of an event that incorporates an integer counter which can be incremented or decremented by multiple interacting threads. The semaphore internally supplies the synchronization needed to ensure that its counter is safely updated without corruption even if several threads attempt to modify it simultaneously. Chapter 5 details the working of semaphores and provides three examples of their use:

1. resource pool
2. commodity pipeline
3. writer-readers

The first example uses the semaphore to maintain a count of the number of (identical) resources in a pool which are currently available to threads competing for these resources. The second example is similar to the 'producer-consumer' example of chapter 4 but here the semaphore provides a count of the commodities currently available to the consumer. The third example is modelled on the common situation where one thread (the 'writer') is allowed to update some resource (data) whilst several threads (the 'readers') can examine the resource but not modify it — the semaphore counts the number of readers.

Chapter 7 covers various techniques that allow different threads to perform thread-specific processing even though they are executing the same code — in particular, the thread synchronization topics of 'keys' and 'one-time initialization' are discussed. A key provides thread-specific storage and essentially acts as a variable which assumes different values when used by different threads. One-time initialization ensures that if several threads can call initialization code which must execute exactly once then the code is actually only executed by whichever thread happens to invoke it first.

1.4 Programming in C++

The C++ language supports object-oriented programming. An 'object' in C++ comprises a data structure describing the object's state together with a collection of functions that define the capabilities of the object — the current state typically determines the exact processing to be performed by the object whenever the functions are invoked. In fact each C++ object belongs to a particular 'class' and all objects in that class share the same set of functions — the individual objects within the class are distinguished by their own independent data. The following chapters will define a variety of C++ object classes that are useful for multi-threaded programming — chapter 2 introduces the fundamental THREAD class whilst later chapters deal with thread synchronization classes such as MUTEX, EVENT and SEMAPHORE.

Many C++ programs use objects in a passive way, merely invoking the functions of an object to obtain the required services. However, with multiple threads it is possible to make an object more active by running one or more internal threads within the object. Chapter 6 discusses these two contrasting approaches in more detail by examining a pair of multiplexer-demultiplexer objects that allow several communication channels to share a common link. Chapter 10 provides an extended example of the process of creating a multi-threaded C++ application in order to illustrate some of the techniques described throughout the book in a more realistic setting.

A class in C++ generalizes the notion of a data structure defined in the C language using the **struct** keyword — the declaration of a class includes function declarations in addition to the data field declarations. For example:

```
class MUTEX {
public:
  MUTEX(void);
  ~MUTEX(void);
  void Acquire(void);
  void Release(void);
private:
  HANDLE Mutex;
};
```

Here the class name is MUTEX and the data structure of each MUTEX object consists of the single field Mutex of type HANDLE — the data in this case is a pointer (or 'handle') to a mutex supplied by the operating system. The class also provides each MUTEX object with four functions: Acquire(), Release(), MUTEX() and ~MUTEX(). Typically the keyword **public** is applied to the class functions whilst the keyword **private** is applied to the class data fields — an object's functions may thus be invoked by external code whilst the internal state remains hidden. The Acquire() and Release() functions are called whenever a thread wants to acquire or release its hold on the mutex. The MUTEX() function is a 'constructor' function for the MUTEX class and the ~MUTEX() function is the corresponding 'destructor' function — a constructor always has the same name as its class and the destructor always prepends the ~ character to this name. The constructor and destructor functions are not usually called explicitly. Instead the constructor is implicitly invoked whenever an object is created and the destructor is implicitly invoked whenever the object is destroyed. The constructor is used to initialize the state of the object and acquire the resources the object will need to operate correctly — the destructor releases those resources which the object still holds when it is destroyed. For a statically declared object, its lifetime extends from the point at which its declaration statement is encountered until the block containing this declaration is exited. For example, here is the declaration of a MUTEX object called mutex contained within a block delimited by enclosing curly brackets:

```
{
       .
       .
   MUTEX mutex; // constructor invoked
       .
       .
   mutex.Acquire();
       .
       .
   mutex.Release();
       .
       .
} // destructor invoked
```

The MUTEX() constructor function is called when program control reaches the declaration statement and the ~MUTEX() destructor function is called when control exits from the block — in between the object's Acquire() and Release() functions may be invoked using the . operator after the object name. For dynamically created objects the lifetime is defined by **new** and **delete** calls — the **new** operator creates the object and returns a pointer to it whilst the **delete** operator takes the pointer and destroys the object.

```
MUTEX* mutex = new MUTEX; // constructor invoked
   .
   .
mutex->Acquire();
   .
   .
mutex->Release();
   .
   .
delete mutex; // destructor invoked
```

The constructor and destructor functions are again called implicitly but now the object's other functions must be invoked by using the -> operator with the pointer returned from the new operation.

1.5 Multi-Threading Implementations

In the following chapters the early sections describe multi-threaded programming in a generic manner and hide the implementation details within the various C++ classes presented there. The later sections in each chapter show how these classes can be implemented using the multi-threading facilities provided by two popular operating systems (UNIX and Windows). This approach is intended to provide a clear understanding of the basic principles whilst still permitting easy application of the material to real-world situations. The UNIX operating system has many different variants and so to provide a good measure of portability the sections relating to UNIX discuss the multi-threading functions defined under the POSIX (Portable Operating System Interface for UNIX) standard. The sections on Windows implementation cover the thread related mechanisms supported by the Win32 Application Programming Interface (API) — the code is specific to Windows 95/98 but should require minimal modification to run under Windows NT. There are, of course, other multi-threading implementations but hopefully the reader will have little difficulty in transferring the knowledge acquired here.

1.6 Summary

Traditionally, most C/C++ applications have used a single thread to perform all the processing required by the program — if several tasks needed to be executed simultaneously the solution usually involved multiple processes each running a single thread. The advent of multi-threaded programming allows the benefits of multi-tasking to be provided within a single process — this is typically much less demanding on system resources than the multi-process equivalent. This chapter has presented an introduction to the fundamentals of multi-threaded programming in the C++ language and has also described the thread synchronization primitives (mutex, event, semaphore) available to coordinate several concurrently executing threads. A 'mutex' provides arbitration amongst a number of threads competing for a shared resource. An 'event' allows one thread to signal that something has happened and another thread to wait for this signal — events permit cooperating threads to regulate their interaction. A 'semaphore' is a generalization of an event that incorporates a built-in counter — the semaphore internally supplies the synchronization to prevent corruption of the counter. C++ classes can be used to package both threads and the synchronization primitives — later chapters introduce the THREAD, MUTEX, EVENT and SEMAPHORE classes. Each C++ class provides a blue-print for creating all of the objects which belong to that class — in particular, the class defines the data structure held by each object and also describes the functionality supported by each of the objects. The lifetime of a C++ object is accurately defined — at creation the class constructor function is called to initialize the new object and at destruction the corresponding destructor is invoked to perform any clean-up processing that may be necessary. Multi-threading and C++ make for a good partnership — C++ allows multi-threading techniques to be applied uniformly across a number of different implementations with irrelevant details being hidden within C++ classes whilst multiple threads enable C++ objects to become active entities in a way that is not possible with a single-threaded approach.

2. Threads

A multi-threaded program typically executes as a collection of threads bundled together within a process. Usually there are more threads active in the system than there are processors on which these threads may run and so some scheduling scheme must be applied to allocate slices of processor time to each thread — provided that every thread is regularly assigned to some processor then all the threads appear to be running concurrently. The threads within a particular process share a common environment that allows them to communicate easily but each thread also maintains a thread-specific context that is not shared. Whenever the thread running on a particular processor is switched, the context of the interrupted thread is recorded and the previously saved context of the newly activated thread is restored. This chapter explains thread scheduling and the thread environment in more detail — the main topics covered are:

— time-slicing and the scheduler
— shared process environment
— thread-specific context
— the THREAD class
— implementation details for UNIX and Windows

The chapter also presents a multi-lingual variant of the traditional Hello program as an introduction to multi-threaded programming.

2.1 Thread Scheduling

A computer program is executed by the computer's central processing unit (CPU) or 'processor' — a multi-tasking system can increase the available computing power by sharing out the workload amongst multiple processors. In any case many multi-threaded applications will run on computers with fewer processors than are required to assign each thread its own dedicated processor — consequently, threads in a multi-threaded application must time-share the available processors. The 'scheduler' forms part of the operating system (or thread library) and it is responsible for allocating processor time to those threads which are currently active in the system. A common scheduling policy is simply to cycle through the set of active threads — to prevent a particular thread from monopolizing processor time, the technique of 'time-slicing' is usually applied. With time-slicing the scheduler allocates each thread a slice of time (around twenty milliseconds) in which to run — at the end of this time-slice the scheduler interrupts the current thread, adds it to the end of a queue and runs another thread from the head of the queue. Thread priorities may be implemented using several different queues — threads from a higher-priority queue are scheduled in preference to those from a lower priority queue.

The following figure illustrates the various states through which each thread progresses during its lifetime:

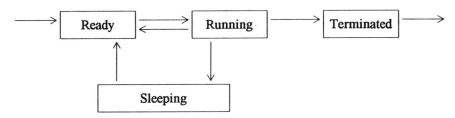

When the thread is created it enters the 'Ready' state — thereafter, the thread moves to the 'Running' state when the scheduler allocates it some processor time and then returns to the 'Ready' state whenever it is interrupted by the scheduler at the end of a time slice. Sometimes the thread must delay further execution for a fixed period of time or until some event occurs — the thread then enters the 'Sleeping' state and is not allocated processor time by the scheduler until it returns to the 'Ready' state. Finally, when the thread has completed its processing it moves to the 'Terminated' state and remains there until it is destroyed by the operating system — other threads can detect that the thread is in the 'Terminated' state for the purpose of thread synchronization.

The scheduler runs each of the active threads in turn and at the end of an allotted time-slice it makes a 'context switch' to transfer control to the next thread. The following figure illustrates the basic procedure involved on a computer with a single processor:

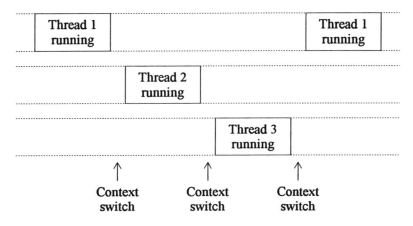

Each context switch involves storing the context of the currently executing thread and restoring the previously saved context of the newly scheduled thread — the context of each thread includes sufficient information on the state of the system to allow the thread to resume execution at the point where it was last interrupted. After the context switch the new thread has control of the processor and the old thread is passively waiting in the 'Ready' state for the next time that the scheduler will allocate it a processor. The following section discusses the context of a thread in more detail.

2.2 Thread Environment

Threads exist within the environment of a process — part of this environment is shared by all threads belonging to the process whilst the remainder is specific to individual threads. The following figure illustrates the various components of the thread environment:

Process

Thread 1	Thread 2	Thread 3
Stack	Stack	Stack
Registers	Registers	Registers
Keys	Keys	Keys

Code
Static Storage
Dynamic Storage

The shared environment comprises executable code, static storage and dynamic storage whilst the thread-specific context comprises stack storage, CPU registers and user-defined keys. In particular, since all threads share the program's executable code it is possible for more than one thread to be executing the same piece of code at the same time. The remaining elements of the thread environment all principally contain data — managing the manipulation of these data structures by a collection of interacting threads is the key to successful multi-threading.

Data in static storage is declared as global variables and exists the whole time that the program is running. Static storage is shared so if several threads use the same data in static storage they must synchronize their activities to prevent data corruption. On the other hand data held in a thread's stack is specific to an individual thread — the stack forms part of the thread context and is switched whenever a new thread is allocated processor time. Every time a thread makes a function call extra space is allocated from its stack to hold the 'stack frame' for the function — the stack frame contains function parameters, local variables declared within the function and also the address of the code that invoked the function so that the thread knows where to resume execution when it returns from the function.

The following figure illustrates how stack space is allocated whenever a function call is made and then deallocated after the function returns:

Before Call	During Call	After Call
Free Space	Free Space	Free Space
	Stack Frame	
Used Space	Used Space	Used Space

Since the stack forms part of each thread context, different threads can simultaneously execute the same function without fear of modifying one another's function parameters and local variables.

Data in the registers (memory cells within the CPU) also forms part of the thread-specific context and is updated during a context switch. The scheduler may interrupt an active thread at any point in its execution so the next program instruction to be executed by this thread must be remembered — the relevant address within the program code is held in a CPU register.

Data held in dynamic memory is allocated using the C++ **new** operator which returns a pointer to the newly allocated memory — the memory may later be deallocated by applying the **delete** operator to this pointer. Dynamic data may belong to either the shared process environment or the thread-specific context depending on how the pointer is held. If the pointer is held in static storage then the dynamic memory is a shared resource — however, if the pointer is held in a thread's stack then the dynamic memory is effectively thread-specific. For example:

```
OBJECT* global_object;

void Function(void) {
  global_object = new OBJECT;
  OBJECT* local_object = new OBJECT;
            .
            .
  delete local_object;
}
```

Here the global_object pointer references an object which can be shared by other threads — however, the local_object pointer is held in the stack frame of the current thread and so references an object which is specific to that thread. The local_object pointer is lost whenever the function returns so the object which it references must be deleted within the function. This technique is often necessary when allocating large temporary structures. The advantage over using a local variable is that only the pointer appears in the function stack frame and the object is allocated in dynamic storage — stack space is typically much smaller than that available for dynamic storage.

The two methods of using dynamic storage just described allow for either long-lived shared data or short-lived thread-specific data. To provide long-lived thread-specific dynamic data, the thread-context may be extended by creating user-defined keys — these are essentially static pointers to dynamic memory which are thread-specific. Chapter 7 discusses the use of keys in much more detail.

2.3 The THREAD Class

The THREAD class is defined to provide generic support for threads. The THREAD class has the following specification:

```
class THREAD {
public:
  THREAD(void);
  virtual ~THREAD(void);
  int Start(void* = NULL);
  void Detach(void);
  void* Wait(void);
  void Stop(void);
  unsigned int GetThreadID(void);
  static unsigned int GetCurrentThreadID(void);
  static void Sleep(int);
protected:
  virtual void* Run(void*);
        .
        .
};
```

This class specification only defines the interface used by external code to work with threads. The internal implementation of the THREAD class is dependent on the operating system — sections 2.5 and 2.6 provide typical implementations for UNIX and Windows operating systems.

The THREAD class Start() function is called to start the thread associated with a THREAD object — each THREAD object corresponds to exactly one thread. The Start() function then invokes the Run() function — this acts as the 'thread function' (analogous to main() for the primary thread) and defines all processing performed by the thread. The Run() function receives the void* parameter originally passed to Start() and this may be used to individualize the actions of different threads — the value of the parameter defaults to NULL if it is not explicitly specified. When Run() eventually completes its processing, the function returns a **void*** value and the thread then enters its 'Terminated' state where it remains until it is destroyed. Another thread may wait for the thread's return value by calling Wait () on the associated THREAD object — alternatively if the return value is unwanted then the Detach () function must be called to allow the operating system to destroy the thread as soon as it terminates. The Detach () function can be called before or after Start () — once a thread has been detached, the Wait () and Stop () functions do not work. The Stop () function is provided to abruptly terminate a thread but, if possible, its use should be avoided in favour of more controlled methods.

Every thread is assigned a unique ID which can be retrieved by calling the GetThreadID () function of the associated THREAD object. The function GetCurrentThreadID () is static and so can be called without reference to a particular THREAD object — the function returns the ID of the thread which calls the function. Finally, the Sleep () function is provided to allow a thread to pause its execution for a specified number of milliseconds — this function moves the thread to the 'Sleeping' state.

2.4 The Hello Program

The Hello program is a good place to start for any new programming language or operating system — however, the traditional Hello program is essentially a single-threaded application so a multi-lingual variant of the Hello program is used here to demonstrate multi-threading techniques. The first step is to derive a new HELLO class from the THREAD base class and define its Run () function — the hello.h header file is simple:

```
hello.h:

#ifndef _HELLO_HEADER
#define _HELLO_HEADER

#include "thread.h"

class HELLO : public THREAD {
protected:
    virtual void* Run(void*);
};

#endif
```

The use of compiler directives such as those involving _HELLO_HEADER helps to simplify the inclusion of header files by automatically preventing multiple declarations of the same item. The Run () function is 'virtual' and so can be overridden in the derived HELLO class — the THREAD class version of the Run () function simply returns immediately. The hello.cxx file provides the definition of the HELLO class function — the extension .cxx applies to C++ source files with alternatives .cpp and .cc and .C also being common.

The `hello.cxx` file contains the following code:

```
hello.cxx:

#include "os.h"
#include <stdio.h>
#include "hello.h"

void* HELLO::Run(void* param) {
  char* message = (char*)param;
  for (int i=0; i<3; i++) {
    printf("%s\n", message);
    Sleep(100);
  }
  return NULL;
}
```

The `os.h` header file hides operating system dependencies — for Windows it simply includes the standard system-defined header `<windows.h>` whereas for UNIX it allows common constants such as `NULL`, `FALSE` and `TRUE` to be provided by the user-defined `unix.h` header. The `stdio.h` header is a system-defined header which is available under both Windows and UNIX — this header is needed in order to use the `printf()` function. The HELLO class `Run()` function treats its initialization parameter as a pointer to a string which is printed to the screen three times at intervals of a tenth of a second. The `Run()` function will be invoked simultaneously by three different threads and each thread will pass in a different message. The `main()` function is assigned the task of creating the THREAD objects and running the associated threads:

```
main.cxx:

#include <stdio.h>
#include "hello.h"

int main(int argc, char** argv) {
  HELLO thread_english;
  HELLO thread_french;
  HELLO thread_german;
  thread_english.Start("Hello");
  thread_french.Start("Bonjour");
  thread_german.Start("Guten Tag");
  thread_english.Wait();
  thread_french.Wait();
  thread_german.Wait();
  printf("Goodbye\n");
  return 0;
}
```

The `main()` function creates the three THREAD objects `thread_english`, `thread_french` and `thread_german` and then calls their `Start()` function with the appropriate greetings. The primary thread then waits for each of the secondary threads to terminate before printing out a farewell message and exiting itself. The exact ordering of thread execution is in general unpredictable but the following output is typical:

```
Hello
Bonjour
Guten Tag
Hello
Bonjour
Guten Tag
Hello
Bonjour
Guten Tag
Goodbye
```

As well as providing an example of deriving a new thread class from the base THREAD class this simple application demonstrates the following multi-threading techniques:

1. passing initialization parameters to identical threads to specialize their behaviours

2. coordinating the activities of a collection of slave threads with one master thread

2.5 UNIX Implementation

This section shows how to implement the THREAD class on a UNIX system which supports the POSIX standard for multi-threading functions such as the `pthread_create()` function. The THREAD class under UNIX acquires the following basic additions:

```
static void* ThreadFunction(void*);

class THREAD {
friend void* ThreadFunction(void*);
          .
          .
private:
  pthread_t ThreadHandle;
  unsigned int ThreadID;
};
```

The implementation of the THREAD class for the Windows operating system acquires similar additions. The `ThreadFunction()` function is called by `Start()` and in turn calls `Run()` — it is required because the thread creation function provided by the operating system must be supplied with a global thread function rather than one belonging to a C++ class. The `ThreadFunction()`

function is made a 'friend' of the THREAD class so that it may call the protected Run() function — the Run() function is otherwise only available to the THREAD class and any derived thread classes. The ThreadFunction() function is declared as static to prevent it from being called directly by external code. The thread associated with the THREAD object is identified by both a ThreadHandle and a ThreadID — the former is an opaque structure that is used only within the THREAD class whereas the latter is simply an unsigned integer retrievable with the function GetThreadID(). The full specification for the THREAD class under UNIX appears in the thread.h header file:

```
thread.h:

#ifndef _THREAD_HEADER
#define _THREAD_HEADER

#include "unix.h"
#include <pthread.h>

static void* ThreadFunction(void*);

class THREAD {
friend void* ThreadFunction(void*);
public:
  THREAD(void);
  virtual ~THREAD(void);
  int Start(void* = NULL);
  void Detach(void);
  void* Wait(void);
  void Stop(void);
  unsigned int GetThreadID(void);
  static unsigned int GetCurrentThreadID(void);
  static void Sleep(int);
protected:
  virtual void* Run(void*);
private:
  pthread_t ThreadHandle;
  unsigned int ThreadID;
  int Started;
  int Detached;
  void* Param;
};

#endif
```

The pthread.h header file supplies all the necessary declarations for working with POSIX threads — in particular, this header file defines the pthread_t type used for the ThreadHandle field.

The `thread.cxx` source file provides the implementation of the THREAD class:

```
thread.cxx:

#include "unix.h"
#include <pthread.h>
#include <sys/time.h>
#include "thread.h"

THREAD::THREAD(void) {
  Started = FALSE;
  Detached = FALSE;
}

THREAD::~THREAD(void) {
  Stop();
}
```

The THREAD() constructor function initializes the `Started` and `Detached` fields when the THREAD object is created. The ~THREAD() destructor function is invoked at object destruction and forcefully stops the associated thread if it is still running and has not been detached. The `Start()`, `ThreadFunction()` and `Run()` functions set the associated thread in motion:

```
int THREAD::Start(void* param) {
  if (!Started) {
    pthread_attr_t attributes;
    pthread_attr_init(&attributes);
    if (Detached)
      pthread_attr_setdetachstate(&attributes,
                          PTHREAD_CREATE_DETACHED);
    Param = param;
    ThreadID = 0;
    if (pthread_create(&ThreadHandle,&attributes,
                          ThreadFunction,this) == 0)
      Started = TRUE;
    pthread_attr_destroy(&attributes);
  }
  return Started;
}

static void* ThreadFunction(void* object) {
  THREAD* thread = (THREAD*)object;
  return thread->Run(thread->Param);
}
```

The `pthread_create()` function actually creates a new thread and also fills in the `ThreadHandle` field. The newly created thread starts to execute the function `ThreadFunction()` and receives a pointer to the THREAD object as a parameter — this pointer is used to call the object's `Run()` function with the parameter originally passed to the Start() function. The base class version of the Run() function performs no processing:

```
void* THREAD::Run(void* param) {
  return NULL;
}
```

The return value from the Run() function is passed back to the operating system via ThreadFunction() and may subsequently be retrieved by calling Wait(). If the Detach() function has been called prior to invoking Start() then the attributes structure is used to start up the new thread in a pre-detached state. The Detach() and Wait() functions are defined as follows:

```
void THREAD::Detach(void) {
  if (Started && !Detached)
    pthread_detach(ThreadHandle);
  Detached = TRUE;
}

void* THREAD::Wait(void) {
  void* status = NULL;
  if (Started && !Detached) {
    pthread_join(ThreadHandle,&status);
    Detached = TRUE;
  }
  return status;
}
```

Note that the Wait() function automatically detaches the thread. The Stop() function abruptly terminates the thread if it is still running and has not previously been detached:

```
void THREAD::Stop(void) {
  if (Started && !Detached) {
    pthread_cancel(ThreadHandle);
    pthread_detach(ThreadHandle);
    Detached = TRUE;
  }
}
```

The ThreadID field as well as the functions GetThreadID() and GetCurrentThreadID() are not implemented here since the POSIX standard provides no direct mechanism — the standard does provide the functions pthread_self() and pthread_equal() for identifying threads but these deal with opaque `pthread_t` handles. Chapter 7 discusses one possible alternative involving thread-specific keys — in the meanwhile a pair of dummy definitions will suffice:

```
unsigned int THREAD::GetThreadID(void) {
  return ThreadID;
}

unsigned int THREAD::GetCurrentThreadID(void) {
  return 0;
}
```

The `Sleep()` function is implemented by causing the `select()` function to timeout after a specified number of milliseconds — the `select()` function is not part of the POSIX threads standard but is commonly available on UNIX systems.

```
void THREAD::Sleep(int delay) {
  timeval timeout = {(delay/1000),
                     ((delay*1000)%1000000)};
  select(0,
    (fd_set*)NULL,(fd_set*)NULL,(fd_set*)NULL,&timeout);
}
```

2.6 Windows Implementation

This section discusses how to implement the THREAD class on a Windows system — as for the UNIX implementation the THREAD class acquires the following basic additions:

```
static unsigned int __stdcall ThreadFunction(void*);

class THREAD {
friend unsigned int __stdcall ThreadFunction(void*);

    .
    .
private:
  HANDLE ThreadHandle;
  unsigned int ThreadID;
};
```

Here the `ThreadFunction()` function must be explicitly declared to use the __stdcall calling convention — the `main()` function uses the default __cdecl calling convention. The thread function returns an unsigned integer value but this can be cast to and from a **void*** pointer value since both are 32-bit quantities under Windows.

The full specification for the THREAD class under Windows appears in the thread.h header file — the windows.h header file supplies all the necessary declarations for working with Windows:

```
thread.h:

#ifndef _THREAD_HEADER
#define _THREAD_HEADER

#include <windows.h>

static unsigned int __stdcall ThreadFunction(void*);

class THREAD {
friend unsigned int __stdcall ThreadFunction(void*);
public:
  THREAD(void);
  virtual ~THREAD(void);
  int Start(void* = NULL);
  void Detach(void);
  void* Wait(void);
  void Stop(void);
  unsigned int GetThreadID(void);
  static unsigned int GetCurrentThreadID(void);
  static void Sleep(int);
protected:
  virtual void* Run(void*);
private:
  HANDLE ThreadHandle;
  unsigned int ThreadID;
  BOOL Started;
  BOOL Detached;
  void* Param;
};

#endif
```

The THREAD class constructor and destructor functions and the THREAD class Run() function are identical to those defined in the previous section for the UNIX implementation — however, the Start() and ThreadFunction() functions are modified slightly. The Windows operating system actually provides a CreateThread() function for thread creation but the (essentially equivalent) function _beginthreadex() must be substituted if the C run-time library is to be called by the program. The thread creation function sets both the ThreadHandle and ThreadID fields of the associated THREAD object — the functions GetThreadID() and GetCurrentThreadID() are easy to implement under Windows.

The `thread.cxx` source file provides the implementation of the THREAD class:

```
thread.cxx:

#include <windows.h>
#include <process.h>
#include "thread.h"

      .
      .
      .

int THREAD::Start(void* param) {
  if (!Started) {
    Param = param;
    if (ThreadHandle =
         (HANDLE)_beginthreadex(NULL,0,
             ThreadFunction,this,0,&ThreadID)) {
      if (Detached)
        CloseHandle(ThreadHandle);
      Started = TRUE;
    }
  }
  return Started;
}

static unsigned int
        __stdcall ThreadFunction(void* object) {
  THREAD* thread = (THREAD*)object;
  return (unsigned int)thread->Run(thread->Param);
}
```

The `process.h` header file is required for the _beginthreadex() function.
The **void*** return value from the Run() function must be cast to an unsigned
integer before being passed back from ThreadFunction() — the Wait()
function recasts the value to a **void*** pointer again:

```
void* THREAD::Wait(void) {
  DWORD status = (DWORD)NULL;
  if (Started && !Detached) {
    WaitForSingleObject(ThreadHandle,INFINITE);
    GetExitCodeThread(ThreadHandle,&status);
    CloseHandle(ThreadHandle);
    Detached = TRUE;
  }
  return (void*)status;
}
```

The Detach() and Stop() functions are implemented as follows:

```
void THREAD::Detach(void) {
  if (Started && !Detached)
    CloseHandle(ThreadHandle);
  Detached = TRUE;
}

void THREAD::Stop(void) {
  if (Started && !Detached) {
    TerminateThread(ThreadHandle,0);
    CloseHandle(ThreadHandle);
    Detached = TRUE;
  }
}
```

Windows provides thread ID values directly so the GetThreadID() and GetCurrentThreadID() functions are straightforward:

```
unsigned int THREAD::GetThreadID(void) {
  return ThreadID;
}

unsigned int THREAD::GetCurrentThreadID(void) {
  return GetCurrentThreadId();
}
```

The THREAD class Sleep() function simply calls the operating system Sleep() function using the :: operator to bypass the identically named class function:

```
void THREAD::Sleep(int delay) {
  ::Sleep(delay);
}
```

2.7 Summary

During its lifetime a thread progresses through a number of different states. Initially the thread enters the 'Ready' state — thereafter it moves between 'Ready' and 'Running' states as the scheduler periodically allocates processor time to the thread. Occasionally the thread may enter the 'Sleeping' state whilst it is waiting for a specified delay to elapse or for some event to occur. Eventually the thread will complete its processing and move to the 'Terminated' state. The thread will remain in this state until it is detached or until another thread calls Wait() to obtain its return value — the operating system will then destroy the thread. Whenever the scheduler allocates a new thread to a processor, a context switch is performed to replace the context of the interrupted thread with that of the newly activated thread. The thread context contains enough information to transparently continue the thread's processing from the point where it was last interrupted. The thread context includes the thread's stack and the processor registers along with any user-defined keys — in particular, the stack holds function parameters and local variables. In addition to the thread-specific data in the thread context, each thread also shares the resources of the process to which it belongs — the process provides shared program code, shared static storage and dynamic storage. The dynamic memory storage may be either shared or partitioned by the process's threads depending on where the pointers to this memory are held. The THREAD class provides a uniform interface to thread facilities independent of the underlying operating system — the implementation of the class contains the system-dependent programming details. A new thread may be started by calling the Start() function of the associated THREAD object — this invokes the ThreadFunction() function which in turn runs the Run() function. Whenever a new thread class is derived from the THREAD base class, the virtual Run() function must be overridden to define the processing required from threads of the new class. The THREAD class functions Detach() and Wait() are provided to detach a thread or to wait for the thread to return an exit code — the Wait() function allows one thread to synchronize its activities with another thread. A thread may be identified by calling the THREAD class GetThreadID() and GetCurrentThreadID() functions — the thread ID is a simple integer value that is unique to each thread. Finally, the Sleep() function allows a thread to move to the 'Sleeping' state for a specified number of milliseconds — in this state the scheduler will not allocate processor time to the thread. This chapter has described typical implementations of the THREAD class for UNIX and Windows operating systems — the Hello program illustrated basic multi-threaded programming through application of the THREAD class.

3. Mutexes

The effectively random nature of thread scheduling introduces a level of unpredictability into the execution of a multi-threaded program — 'thread synchronization' must be provided to help regulate the interaction of the various threads and so prevent these time-dependent variations from affecting the correct operation of the application. This synchronization is provided by primitives such as 'mutexes', 'events' and 'semaphores' that are supported by the operating system — this chapter introduces mutexes whilst the next two chapters cover events and semaphores respectively. The principal purpose of a mutex is to ensure 'mutual exclusion' amongst a number of threads all competing for the same resource — however, this basic function can be applied in a range of different circumstances and these are detailed throughout the chapter. The main topics covered here include:

— thread scheduling and synchronization
— the MUTEX class
— atomic operations
— inter-thread communication
— state transitions and snapshots
— implementation details for UNIX and Windows

The chapter also describes the ATOMIC class as an illustration of 'serializing' the processing performed by several threads which attempt to run simultaneously.

3.1 Why Synchronize?

As described in chapter 2 threads exist within the environment of a process — for each process the principal means of communication between the individual threads is through modification of the shared process environment. However, the scheduler can interrupt the execution of a thread at unpredictable instants and this opens the possibility that one thread may not leave the process environment in a consistent state ready for the next thread to be activated. The solution to this problem is to apply the techniques of 'thread synchronization' to regulate the activities of the interacting threads. Indeed the synchronization primitives such as mutexes, events and semaphores are provided for just this purpose. Generally speaking, a mutex ensures consistency on a small scale (protecting the integrity of a single variable or data structure) whilst events and semaphores are required to coordinate processing of larger elements of the shared environment (for example, signalling when one thread has prepared a buffer of data ready for another thread to use).

The principal application of thread synchronization primitives is consequently to ensure that each modification of the process state is complete before control can be passed to another thread. Since a single modification of the state typically involves a number of more elementary actions it is evident that thread synchronization simply provides a mechanism of grouping a sequence of such actions into an indivisible operation — the synchronization effectively ensures that the entire sequence is 'atomic' and cannot be subdivided by the scheduler. A simple example is provided by the incrementing of a shared counter — this can be useful if, for instance, a sequence of unique ID numbers are to be assigned by various threads. So suppose that no mutex protection is provided for the counter and that threads obtain the current counter value by calling the following function:

```
int GetID(void) {
   return Counter++;
}
```

The exact processing performed by GetID() is dependent on the compiler but typically involves the following steps:

1. store the current value of Counter in some temporary variable
2. increment the value of Counter
3. return the stored value

If two threads concurrently call GetID() with the Counter variable initially holding the value 0, the following sequence of events is possible:

thread A	thread B
·	·
store 0	·
·	store 0
·	increment Counter
·	return 0
increment Counter	·
return 0	·
·	·

Without proper synchronization thread A can store the initial value of the Counter variable and then relinquish control before it has had a chance to increment the counter ready for the thread B. Consequently both threads return the value 0 from the GetID() function. Furthermore, the final value of Counter may be 1 or 2 depending on whether thread A increments the value it originally stored (0) or the current value (1) which is set by thread B. The lack of synchronization clearly introduces an unacceptable level of unpredictability into the processing performed by the program.

Fortunately the remedy is straightforward:

```
int GetID(void) {
  Mutex.Acquire();
  int id = Counter++;
  Mutex.Release();
  return id;
}
```

Here the `Mutex` object is used to provide the necessary synchronization. Now only one thread at a time can execute the code between the `Acquire()` and `Release()` calls — a portion of code bracketed in this way is sometimes referred to as a 'critical region' or 'critical section' but in this book the term 'mutex (protected code) block' is applied. Now if simultaneous calls to `GetID()` are made by threads A and B then whilst thread A is executing the code within the mutex block thread B must wait in the `Acquire()` function. A typical sequence of events might be as follows:

thread A	thread B
.	.
store 0	.
increment Counter	.
.	store 1
.	increment Counter
.	return 1
return 0	.
.	.

There is still some degree of unpredictability but now one thread will always obtain the value 0, the other thread will always obtain the value 1 and the final value of the `Counter` variable will always be 2. The assignment of the values 0 and 1 is determined entirely by the order in which the threads execute the mutex block — in particular, note that the order in which the threads invoke `GetID()` or return from the function call is not the crucial factor. In the last example thread B might well have called `GetID()` before thread A but this did not guarantee that it acquired the mutex first — similarly thread B returned the value 1 before thread A was able to return the value 0.

A final point of interest is the use of the local variable `id` to transfer the current counter value out of the mutex block — the mutex must be released before the `return` statement and so the shared `Counter` variable cannot be referenced there but the thread-specific data held by the `id` variable may safely be read. This is all discussed at greater length in section 3.9 which covers the topic of taking 'snapshots' of shared data.

3.2 Mutex Mechanics

When one thread acquires a mutex all subsequent attempts to acquire the same mutex will block until the first thread releases the mutex. It may be helpful to understand the mechanics of this process as implemented by the operating system (or thread library) — obviously the details will vary between implementations but a conceptual overview will suffice here. So suppose that several threads are competing for a single mutex and that one of the threads has already managed to acquire the mutex. As discussed in section 2.1 when another thread calls `Acquire()` it blocks and moves to the 'Sleeping' state — the thread is then said to be 'sleeping on the mutex'. Whilst the thread is asleep it consumes practically no processor power making this an efficient mechanism for thread synchronization — for example, there is no polling to determine if the mutex has been released. Whenever the first thread eventually does call `Release()` the other thread is awoken and moved to the 'Ready' state ready to compete for the mutex. The following figure illustrates the sequence of events:

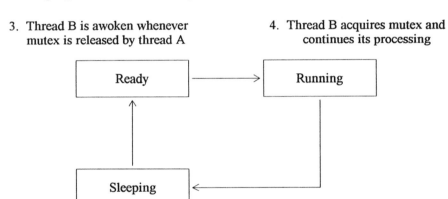

3. Thread B is awoken whenever mutex is released by thread A

4. Thread B acquires mutex and continues its processing

2. Thread B sleeps on mutex

1. Thread B tries to acquire mutex already held by thread A

If there are multiple threads sleeping on the same mutex the operating system will awaken at least one of them — if several threads are awoken it is likely that the majority will soon be put back to sleep. The freshly awoken threads must compete for the mutex in the usual manner and are not guaranteed immediate success — in particular, the released mutex may actually be acquired by another thread that was not sleeping at all but which has just called `Acquire()`. Nonetheless, the operating system does attempt to ensure fairness so that all threads wishing to acquire the mutex will do so eventually.

3.3 The MUTEX Class

The MUTEX class implements the functionality of a mutex as described in the previous sections — the class conceals operating system dependent implementation details and provides a consistent interface to the underlying mutex services by defining five public functions:

```
class MUTEX {
public:
  MUTEX(void);
  virtual ~MUTEX(void);
  virtual void Acquire(void);
  virtual int Acquired(void);
  virtual void Release(void);
     ...
};
```

As explained in section 1.4 MUTEX() and ~MUTEX() are the constructor and destructor functions for the MUTEX class — these functions are called implicitly whenever a MUTEX object is created or destroyed. A thread explicitly calls the Acquire(), Acquired() and Release() functions to acquire or release the mutex packaged within the MUTEX object — after a thread has successfully called Acquire() or Acquired() it then 'holds' the mutex (or equivalently the MUTEX object) until Release() is invoked. Whilst the mutex is held any calls to Acquire() or Acquired() by other threads for the same MUTEX object will fail — the difference between the Acquire() and Acquired() functions is that Acquire() fails by blocking until the mutex can be acquired whilst Acquired() returns immediately with a TRUE or FALSE status value to indicate whether or not the mutex has been acquired. The action of a thread attempting to acquire a mutex which it already holds is implementation dependent. For example, under Windows a thread is always able to reacquire a mutex whereas on POSIX systems the thread is normally blocked while it waits for itself to release the mutex — this latter situation is termed 'deadlock' and represents a specific case of a more general problem discussed in chapter 8. The RECURSIVE_MUTEX class to be introduced in section 8.3 will allow a thread to reliably reacquire a mutex — the RECURSIVE_MUTEX class is derived from the MUTEX class and so the base class functions are made virtual. In the meanwhile it should be assumed for the sake of portability that the action of a thread calling Acquire() for a MUTEX object which it has already acquired is undefined. Similarly if a thread calls Release() for a MUTEX object which it has not acquired then this action is also undefined. Anyway, the proper usage of the MUTEX class is straightforward:

```
class SEQUENCE {
public:
     ...
  int GetID(void);
private:
  MUTEX Mutex;
  int Counter;
};
```

Here the SEQUENCE class provides the GetID() function discussed in section 3.1 — each SEQUENCE object produces its own sequence of unique ID values and so contains a Counter variable together with an associated Mutex object to protect it. The class function is practically identical to the global function from the earlier section:

```
int SEQUENCE::GetID(void) {
  Mutex.Acquire();
  int id = Counter++;
  Mutex.Release();
  return id;
}
```

The GetID() function may be invoked as follows:

thread A	**thread B**
.	.
SEQUENCE sequence;	.
.	.
int id = sequence.GetID();	.
.	.
.	int id = sequence.GetID();
.	.

Once the SEQUENCE object has been created any thread can safely call its GetID() function to obtain a unique ID value. Note that here the sequence object is shared by threads A and B but each thread declares its own id variable.

3.4 Using Mutexes

There are several common situations where a mutex is required:

— atomic operations
— inter-thread communication
— state transitions
— snapshots

The next few sections discuss each of these possibilities in more detail. However, it is worth noting that the coordination amongst threads which synchronization primitives enforce can significantly reduce the efficiency of a program and so unnecessary synchronization should be avoided. Indeed in certain circumstances it may be possible to avoid synchronization by using a single thread or to deduce from the logic of the program that synchronization is not required. For example, there is often only one thread active during program initialization — similarly only a single thread is typically responsible for initializing a particular C++ object.

3.5 Atomic Operations

As discussed in section 3.1 the basic purpose of a mutex is to make a section of code indivisible so that it constitutes an 'atomic operation'. A common technique is to package the mutex block within a function:

```
void NAME::SetName(char* forename,char* surname) {
  Mutex.Acquire();
  strcpy(Forename,forename);
  strcpy(Surname,surname);
  Mutex.Release();
}

void NAME::GetName(char* forename,char* surname) {
  Mutex.Acquire();
  strcpy(forename,Forename);
  strcpy(surname,Surname);
  Mutex.Release();
}
```

Here the Forename and Surname variables can be safely written and read by a number of threads without fear of corruption — the atomicity provided by the mutex protection ensures that the data values always represent pairs supplied by the last thread to successfully call SetName(). Note that in general the GetName() function could not be replaced by separate GetForename() and GetSurname() functions since two calls would then be needed to retrieve the complete name — this breaks the atomicity of the read operation and allows for an intervening SetName() call.

Another possibility is to use the C++ object construction and destruction process to automatically acquire and release a mutex — the Acquire() call is placed in the constructor of an associated RESOURCE object and the Release() call in the corresponding destructor:

```
RESOURCE::RESOURCE(MUTEX* mutex)  : Mutex(mutex) {
  Mutex->Acquire();
}

RESOURCE::~RESOURCE(void) {
  Mutex->Release();
}
```

As described in section 1.4 a C++ object is created and destroyed at well-defined instants with the constructor and destructor being invoked implicitly — hence, all that is needed to automatically acquire and release the mutex is to create and destroy the RESOURCE object at the appropriate points in the program.

For example:

```
{
    RESOURCE resource(Mutex);
        ...
    // thread holds mutex
        ...
}
```

The mutex is acquired when the RESOURCE object is declared and is released whenever the block containing this declaration is exited — note that a new RESOURCE object is created each time the block is executed but it must always be the same mutex that is acquired. This version of the RESOURCE class has the following specification:

```
class RESOURCE {
public:
    RESOURCE(MUTEX*);
    ~RESOURCE(void);
private:
    MUTEX* Mutex;
};
```

The constructor accepts a MUTEX* pointer as a parameter and this is stored in the Mutex field of the RESOURCE object so that it is available within the destructor. An alternative would be to create the MUTEX object using a static field of the RESOURCE class but this approach has the disadvantage that the RESOURCE class cannot be used with several different mutexes each protecting their own section of code. In any case one advantage of the RESOURCE class technique is that it works well with C++ exceptions:

```
try {
    RESOURCE resource(Mutex);
        ...
    if (error)
        throw EXCEPTION();
        ...
}
    catch (EXCEPTION e) {
        ...
}
```

As before if execution exits the **try** block normally (thus by-passing the **catch** block) then the RESOURCE object is destroyed and its mutex is released. However, if the **throw** statement is instead executed, thereby transferring control directly to the error handler in the **catch** block, then the RESOURCE object is again destroyed and the mutex released. All this automation by the C++ language results in very clean code — in a real application with several resources, explicit calls to Acquire() and Release() can easily produce convoluted code.

Using a mutex block to provide atomicity ensures that the enclosed sequence of operations can be performed by only one thread at a time. The effect is to 'serialize' the attempts of various threads trying to simultaneously execute the block — first one thread runs the code then another. To illustrate the process of serialization more fully the following section describes the ATOMIC class — this class permits scheduling of a list of arbitrary operations which can then be executed atomically with respect to all other such lists.

3.6 The ATOMIC Class

The ATOMIC class illustrates some of the uses of mutexes just described — in particular, the class is designed to enable serialization of various atomic operations each consisting of an arbitrary list of actions. The ATOMIC class has the following specification:

```
class ATOMIC {
public:
  ATOMIC(void);
  ~ATOMIC(void);
  int Add(ATOMIC_ACTION*,void* = NULL);
  void Execute(void);
private:
  static MUTEX Mutex;
  ATOMIC_ACTION* Actions[ATOMIC_MAX_ACTIONS];
  void* Params[ATOMIC_MAX_ACTIONS];
  int Count;
};
```

Each thread should create its own ATOMIC object:

```
ATOMIC* atomic = new ATOMIC;
```

The thread then passes the ATOMIC* pointer as a parameter to functions belonging to the interfaces of various other C++ objects. These objects make calls to add actions to the list maintained by the ATOMIC object:

```
atomic->Add(&action,param);
```

Finally, the thread calls the Execute() function to execute the list of actions — the ATOMIC class ensures that this is an atomic operation with respect to the execution of lists constructed by other threads. The ATOMIC object constructor initially empties the list of actions (and the destructor performs no processing):

```
ATOMIC::ATOMIC(void) {
  Count = 0;
}

ATOMIC::~ATOMIC(void) {}
```

The Add() function takes a pointer to an ATOMIC_ACTION object and an optional **void*** parameter with default value NULL — the object defines one action in the list and the exact processing performed can be tailored using the parameter. The Add() function has the following definition:

```
int ATOMIC::Add(ATOMIC_ACTION* action,void* param) {
  int status = FALSE;
  if (Count < ATOMIC_MAX_ACTIONS) {
    Actions[Count] = action;
    Params[Count++] = param;
    status = TRUE;
  }
  return status;
}
```

For simplicity the actions and their parameters are stored in the two arrays Actions and Params and the Add() function returns FALSE if the arrays fill up — a more sophisticated implementation might replace the arrays with an expandable linked list. The Count field contains the current number of actions whilst the maximum number of actions is fixed by the following constant:

```
const int ATOMIC_MAX_ACTIONS = 100;
```

Finally, the Execute() function iterates through the accumulated list of actions and then clears the list ready for the next atomic operation:

```
void ATOMIC::Execute(void) {
  Mutex.Acquire();
  for (int i=0; (i<Count); i++)
    Actions[i]->Execute(Params[i]);
  Count = 0;
  Mutex.Release();
}
```

Whilst the list of actions is being built using Add() no synchronization is necessary because only a single thread is involved — however, the Execute() function achieves serialization amongst all ATOMIC objects by using a mutex block protected by a MUTEX object which (being declared as a static field) belongs to the ATOMIC class as a whole. The ATOMIC class Execute() function calls the Execute() function of each of the ATOMIC_ACTION objects from the list — these objects actually belong to various classes derived from the ATOMIC_ACTION class:

```
class ATOMIC_ACTION {
public:
  virtual void Execute(void*) = 0;
};
```

The ATOMIC_ACTION class specifies a single virtual function giving the types of its parameter and return value — the parameter is a **void*** pointer and the return type is **void**. The marker =0 indicates that the function is 'pure virtual', meaning that the ATOMIC_ACTION class provides no definition of the implementation of the function. The ATOMIC_ACTION class is in fact an 'interface class' since its sole purpose is to specify the functional interface provided by classes derived from the ATOMIC_ACTION class — C++ does not allow objects to be created from interface classes but objects of derived classes are allowed providing that these classes define implementations for all functions in the interface. Here classes derived from ATOMIC_ACTION need only define the Execute() function in order to permit the creation of objects. As an example of using the ATOMIC class suppose that the HELLO class from section 2.4 is modified to print out its greetings one character at a time:

```
void* HELLO::Run(void* param) {
  char* string = (char*)param;
  char letter;
  while (letter = *string++)
    printf("%c",letter);
  printf("\n");
  return NULL;
}
```

The printing of each character constitutes one action but the sequence of actions is not mutex-protected to form an atomic operation — the characters from different greetings will be intermingled. The solution, of course, is to serialize the printing of the various greetings and the first step is to derive a new action class from the ATOMIC_ACTION base class:

```
class HELLO_ACTION : public ATOMIC_ACTION {
public:
  virtual void Execute(void*);
};
```

The HELLO_ACTION class must provide a definition of the Execute() function:

```
void HELLO_ACTION::Execute(void* param) {
  char letter = (char)(long)param;
  printf("%c",letter);
}
```

The action specified is to print a single character — the HELLO class Run() function can now build a list of such actions into an atomic operation.

Each HELLO object embeds an ATOMIC object and a HELLO_ACTION object within itself:

```
class HELLO : public THREAD {
protected:
  virtual void* Run(void*);
private:
  ATOMIC Atomic;
  HELLO_ACTION Action;
};
```

Since the HELLO_ACTION objects carry no data they are all identical and so a single HELLO_ACTION object could be shared by all HELLO objects — the saving in space would be negligible though. The HELLO class Run() function may now be modified to ensure that the printing of the different greetings is properly serialized:

```
void* HELLO::Run(void* param) {
  char* string = (char*)param;
  char letter;
  while (letter = *string++)
    Atomic.Add(Action,letter);
  Atomic.Add(Action,'\n');
  Atomic.Execute();
  return NULL;
}
```

The Atomic object's Add() function is called repeatedly to schedule the list of actions and then its Execute() function is invoked to perform all the actions atomically.

3.7 Inter-Thread Communication

Another common application of mutexes is inter-thread communication. In this situation the mutex is used to protect a block of shared data — in this book the term 'mutex (protected data) block' is applied and the distinction with a 'mutex (protected code) block' is sometimes blurred since the latter typically manipulates the former. The data in a mutex block can provide communications via simple flags or perhaps more complex data structures but basically it serves two functions:

1. it allows one thread to control the actions of another thread
2. it allows one thread to provide information to another thread

An example of the former is using a flag to tell a looping thread when to quit:

```
void* LOOPY::Run(void* param) {
  Mutex.Acquire();
  while (Flag != LOOPY_QUIT) {
    Mutex.Release();
        ...
    Mutex.Acquire();
  }
  Mutex.Release();
  return NULL;
}
```

The `Flag` variable is examined within the mutex block and the thread exits whenever the flag is set to `LOOPY_QUIT` — the control thread performs this action:

```
void LOOPY::Quit(void) {
  Mutex.Acquire();
  Flag = LOOPY_QUIT;
  Mutex.Release();
}
```

An alternative approach using an event to signal that the looping thread should exit is described in section 4.3.

An example of one thread communicating information to another by means of a mutex block is provided by two threads which share a circular data buffer. One thread writes data into the buffer and updates its `Write` pointer whilst the other thread reads data from the buffer and updates its `Read` pointer — the following figure illustrates the arrangement:

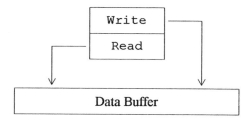

The `Write` and `Read` variables form a control block which may be protected by a mutex. The `BUFFER` class `SetWrite()` function is defined as follows:

```
void BUFFER::SetWrite(int write) {
  Mutex.Acquire();
  Write = write;
  Mutex.Release();
}
```

And the BUFFER class GetWrite() function has the following definition:

```
int BUFFER::GetWrite(void) {
  Mutex.Acquire();
  int write = Write;
  Mutex.Release();
  return write;
}
```

The SetRead() and GetRead() functions are analogous to the SetWrite() and GetWrite() functions. Initially the Write and Read pointers are zeroed to point at the start of the buffer. Thereafter only the writer thread updates the Write variable and so it may read its value directly — however, it must call the SetWrite() and GetRead() functions in order to communicate reliably with the reader thread. Conversely the reader thread can read the Read variable directly but must call the SetRead() and GetWrite() functions. The writer thread is free to write into the buffer between the Write and Read pointers — the amount of space available can be calculated as follows:

```
int space_available = GetRead()-Write;
if (space_available <= 0)
  space_available += BUFFER_SIZE;
```

Similarly the reader thread is free to read from the buffer between the Read and Write pointers — the amount of data available can be calculated as follows:

```
int data_available = GetWrite()-Read;
if (data_available < 0)
  data_available += BUFFER_SIZE;
```

If the Write and Read pointers are identical (as they are initially) this indicates that the buffer is completely empty — however, a full buffer would also make the pointers equal and so this condition must be avoided. Since the two threads always access different regions of the data buffer then only the control block and not the buffer itself need be protected by a mutex. This is an example of the situation mentioned in section 3.4 where program logic can be used to deduce that synchronization is unnecessary. The CLOCK class of section 8.5 provides another variation on the theme of transferring information via a mutex block — in this case an internal TIMER thread periodically updates the Time variable which can then be examined by calling the GetTime() function:

```
void CLOCK::GetTime(int& hour,int& minute,int& second) {
  Mutex.Acquire();
  hour = Time/3600;
  minute = (Time/60)%60;
  second = Time%60;
  Mutex.Release();
}
```

3.8 State Transitions

Yet another application of mutex blocks is to implement 'state transitions' — the mutex ensures that the transition from one state to the next is complete before another thread can take control. A transition is initiated by some stimulus, then decisions are made, actions are executed and finally a new state is entered — the old state, the type of stimulus and the decision process all combine to determine the actions chosen and the new state. The BUFFER class introduced in the previous section provides a good example of state transitions — an outline definition of the BUFFER class WriteData() function is as follows:

```
void BUFFER::WriteData(char* data, int length) {
  int read, space_available;
  int ready = FALSE;
  while (!ready) {
    read = GetRead();
    space_available = read-Write;
    if (space_available <= 0)
      space_available += BUFFER_SIZE;
    if (length < space_available)
      ready = TRUE;
    else {
      Mutex.Acquire();
      if (read == Read) {
        WriterWaiting = TRUE;
        Mutex.Release();
        // wait for space in buffer
      }
      else
        Mutex.Release();
    }
  }
  // copy data into buffer
  int write = (Write+length)%BUFFER_SIZE;
  SetWrite(write);
  // signal reader data is available
}
```

The writer thread remains in the 'Writing' state until the data buffer fills and then it enters the 'Waiting' state until the reader thread makes some space available — the BUFFER class ReadData() function is analogous to WriteData() and the reader thread makes similar transitions to the writer but between 'Reading' and 'Waiting' states. If the writer determines that there is insufficient space to write the data (stimulus) then it sets the WriterWaiting flag (action) and starts to wait (new state) — the WriterWaiting flag tells the reader thread to signal when it has cleared some space in the full buffer. However, as a final check the writer reacquires the mutex and ensures that the reader has not updated its Read variable (decision) — if the Read variable has changed then there is no action and the writer remains in the 'Writing' state. The various state transitions made by the writer and reader threads are illustrated in the following figure:

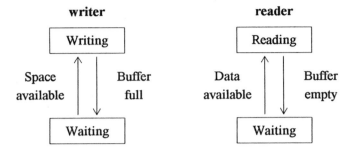

The transition of the writer between Writing and Waiting states actually occurs within the mutex block which checks on the Read variable and not during the calculation of space_available. Since the reader only signals to the writer that it has removed data if the WriterWaiting flag is set, the decision involving the Read variable is essential — without it the writer might find the buffer full and then the reader could read some data without telling the writer thus leaving the writer to wait indefinitely. An alternative approach for the BUFFER class is simply to enclose the whole of the calculation of space_available within the WriteData() function in a mutex block (and similarly the calculation of data_available within the ReadData() function) — it is then sensible to dispense with the four functions SetWrite(), SetRead(), GetWrite() and GetRead(). This approach is illustrated in section 4.4 which describes the modified BUFFER class in full detail.

Another example of a state transition is provided by the LOOPY class Quit() function from the previous section:

```
void LOOPY::Quit(void) {
  Mutex.Acquire();
  Flag = LOOPY_QUIT;
  Mutex.Release();
}
```

Here a transition to the Quit state is made regardless of the current state or indeed of any other conditions — this is often the case when entering a final state.

3.9 Snapshots

A mutex block is sometimes used to copy the current value of shared data into thread-specific storage — this provides the thread with a 'snapshot' of the data. Once the mutex is released the shared data may well be altered by other threads but the snapshot remains fixed — consequently, the thread taking the snapshot can continue its processing without need for further synchronization. The BUFFER class WriteData() function from the previous section provides an example:

```
read = GetRead();
space_available = read-Write;
if (space_available <= 0)
   space_available += BUFFER_SIZE;
```

Here the value of the shared Read field is copied to the local variable read and this is subsequently used to calculate space_available. Once the snapshot is taken the reader thread may update its Read pointer but this does not interfere with the calculations of the writer thread — furthermore, any modification to Read will only be detected whenever the writer takes another snapshot. Thus snapshots can provide a kind of 'double-buffering' with one thread working on the current data whilst another thread is updating the data ready for the next iteration.

Snapshots can be passed around in a variety of ways — for example, the GetRead() function copies the shared Read field into a variable local to the function:

```
int BUFFER::GetRead(void) {
   Mutex.Acquire();
   int read = Read;
   Mutex.Release();
   return read;
}
```

The GetRead() function supplies the snapshot to external code via its return value:

```
read = GetRead();
```

Here the snapshot is transferred to yet another local variable — alternatively the snapshot could be passed into a function as a parameter:

```
space_available = SpaceAvailable(GetRead());
```

The key point throughout is that the snapshot is maintained as part of the thread-specific context (local variable, return value or function parameter) as discussed in section 2.2.

Indeed snapshots find many applications but care must be taken not to confuse one snapshot with the next — for example, suppose that the GetValue() function provides a snapshot of some shared variable and consider the following fragment of code:

```
if (GetValue() == 0)
   printf("%i",GetValue());
```

If another thread changes the value of the shared variable between the two calls to
`GetValue()` the value printed will not be zero as expected. The problem is that
two snapshots are taken when only one would suffice — this can easily be avoided
using a local variable:

```
int value = GetValue();
if (value == 0)
  printf("%i",value);
```

The code fragment will then only ever print out the correct value. Another example
is provided by the BUFFER class `WriteData()` function of the previous section
— in this case the error would be in using one snapshot too long rather than in
using the next snapshot too soon. The check made by the writer thread that the
reader thread has not updated its Read variable is actually a check that the writer
is still using a valid snapshot — the problems would arise if the writer based its
decision to wait upon an out-of-date snapshot.

3.10 UNIX Implementation

The previous few sections have illustrated how to use the MUTEX class — it is now
necessary to discuss the implementation of the MUTEX class for real operating
systems. The POSIX standard for UNIX specifies a `pthread_mutex_t` type that
supports mutex operations — a structure of this type is embedded in each MUTEX
object:

```
mutex.h:

#ifndef _MUTEX_HEADER
#define _MUTEX_HEADER

#include <pthread.h>

class MUTEX {
public:
  MUTEX(void);
  virtual ~MUTEX(void);
  virtual void Acquire(void);
  virtual int Acquired(void);
  virtual void Release(void);
private:
  pthread_mutex_t Mutex;
};

#endif
```

The MUTEX class constructor initializes the Mutex field by calling the pthread_mutex_init() function whilst the destructor calls the function pthread_mutex_destroy() to inform the operating system that the mutex is no longer required:

mutex.cxx:

```
#include "unix.h"
#include "mutex.h"

MUTEX::MUTEX(void) {
  pthread_mutex_init(&Mutex,(pthread_mutexattr_t*)NULL);
}

MUTEX::~MUTEX(void) {
  pthread_mutex_destroy(&Mutex);
}
```

The NULL parameter passed to pthread_mutex_init() specifies a standard mutex with default attributes. The Acquire(), Acquired() and Release() functions are also straightforward to implement by making the appropriate calls to the pthread_mutex_lock(), pthread_mutex_trylock() and pthread_mutex_unlock() functions provided by the operating system:

```
  void MUTEX::Acquire(void) {
    pthread_mutex_lock(&Mutex);
  }

  int MUTEX::Acquired(void) {
    return (pthread_mutex_trylock(&Mutex) == 0);
  }

  void MUTEX::Release(void) {
    pthread_mutex_unlock(&Mutex);
  }
```

Indeed the MUTEX class basically provides wrappers for the mutex functions supported by POSIX — the great advantage is that all the details are hidden behind a consistent interface and this assists portability to other operating systems.

3.11 Windows Implementation

The implementation of the MUTEX class under Windows is very similar to that described in the previous section — however, here each MUTEX object embeds a mutex handle of generic type HANDLE rather than a pthread_mutex_t structure:

```
mutex.h:

#ifndef _MUTEX_HEADER
#define _MUTEX_HEADER

#include <windows.h>

class MUTEX {
public:
   MUTEX(void);
   virtual ~MUTEX(void);
   virtual void Acquire(void);
   virtual int Acquired(void);
   virtual void Release(void);
private:
   HANDLE Mutex;
};

#endif
```

Under Windows the MUTEX class constructor calls CreateMutex() to obtain a handle that references a newly created mutex whilst the destructor releases the mutex by calling CloseHandle() for this handle:

```
mutex.cxx:

#include <windows.h>
#include "mutex.h"

MUTEX::MUTEX(void) {
   Mutex = CreateMutex(NULL,FALSE,NULL);
}

MUTEX::~MUTEX(void) {
   CloseHandle(Mutex);
}
```

The first parameter to the CreateMutex() function deals with security and need only be specified under Windows NT (for Windows 98 it is set to NULL) whilst the third parameter is NULL to request a nameless mutex (using a name allows a mutex to be shared amongst processes). Similar parameters appear in the creation functions for the other synchronization primitives provided by Windows. Finally, the second parameter to CreateMutex() is FALSE to indicate that the mutex is initially not acquired by the thread creating the mutex. The MUTEX class Acquire() and Acquired() functions are implemented using the general purpose function WaitForSingleObject() — chapter 2 showed how this function can be used to detect the termination of a Windows thread and later chapters will detail its use with Windows events and semaphores.

```
void MUTEX::Acquire(void) {
  WaitForSingleObject(Mutex,INFINITE);
}

int MUTEX::Acquired(void) {
  return (WaitForSingleObject(Mutex,0)!=WAIT_TIMEOUT);
}
```

The second parameter to `WaitForSingleObject()` specifies a timeout period after which the function will return if it fails to acquire the mutex — for the blocking function the timeout is infinite whilst for the non-blocking function it is zero. The MUTEX class `Release()` function simply calls the `ReleaseMutex()` function provided by Windows:

```
void MUTEX::Release(void) {
  ReleaseMutex(Mutex);
}
```

3.12 Summary

Synchronization primitives allow a program to manage the unpredictability introduced by the scheduler as it allocates processor time first to one thread and then another — in particular, a mutex prevents one thread from being interrupted by another whilst it is executing a block of code protected by the mutex. The MUTEX class packages each mutex provided by the operating system within an associated MUTEX object — specific implementations for Windows and UNIX systems have been described. The MUTEX class functions `Acquire()` and `Release()` allow external code to acquire and release its hold on the embedded mutex. Once one thread has acquired a particular mutex any other thread which calls `Acquire()` for the same MUTEX object will block until the first thread calls `Release()` — the blocked threads all enter an efficient 'Sleeping' state. The basic service provided by the MUTEX class is therefore mutual exclusion but this can be applied in a number of different situations: atomic operations, inter-thread communication, state transitions and snapshots. A sequence of actions protected by a mutex become an indivisible atomic operation — if several threads all simultaneously attempt to execute atomic operations protected by the same mutex then the processing will be serialized so that the threads execute their mutex blocks one after another. The C++ object construction and destruction process can be used to partially automate the implementation of an atomic operation whereas the ATOMIC class illustrates an alternative approach based upon the C++ notion of an 'interface class' — interface classes do not permit object creation directly but instead supply a specification for the functional interface which must be implemented by the derived classes that actually will supply the objects. Inter-thread communication can be used simply to transfer information or alternatively to allow one thread to control the actions of another — typically the communication occurs via shared data within the process environment with mutex protection required to prevent corruption and so enable reliable interaction between the threads. Mutex protection is also invaluable whenever a thread is updating the state of an application — in this situation some stimulus causes the thread to take various decisions and, depending upon the outcome, it will then execute certain actions and make a transition from the old state to some new state. A thread may also decide to take a 'snapshot' of the current state by copying it into thread-specific storage under the protection of a mutex — providing that the snapshot remains valid the thread can continue its processing without need for further synchronization even if the shared state is concurrently updated by another thread. Thread synchronization is indeed an important part of multi-threaded programming but it can be inefficient and should be avoided whenever possible — sometimes only a single thread is involved in a particular task or the logic of the program can be used to deduce that synchronization is unnecessary.

4. Events

Mutexes prevent different threads from stepping on each other's toes while events allow them to dance in harmony with one another — mutexes and events together encompass all the thread synchronization facilities necessary for multi-threaded programming. Indeed the next chapter shows how mutexes and events can be combined to create semaphores, another essential building block for thread synchronization. An event provides an efficient mechanism for coordinating the activities of cooperating threads — one thread signals that an event has occurred and another thread waits quietly for the signal without wasting valuable processor power in polling. This two-handed communication between threads allows the order in which the various threads execute their code to be precisely regulated by the program — mutex protection, on the other hand, does not make any promises regarding the thread serialization sequence. The key topics covered by this chapter include:

— automatic and manual events
— the EVENT class
— the 'producer-consumer' paradigm
— implementation details for UNIX and Windows

The chapter also describes the TIC_TAC_TOE class which plays a mean game of noughts-and-crosses — this example illustrates how to schedule a background thread to perform lengthy computations whilst leaving the foreground thread responsive for user interaction.

4.1 Event Basics

An event enables one thread to signal to one or more other threads that something has happened — the execution of the other threads is temporarily blocked while they wait for the event to be signalled. Thus an event allows cooperating threads to coordinate their activities, whereas a mutex is used to arbitrate amongst a number of competing threads. However, despite their differences, mutexes and events have much in common and a mutex can be forced to function as an event:

thread A	thread B
.	.
`mutex.Acquire();`	.
.	`mutex.Release();`
.	.

Here thread A calls `Acquire()` for a MUTEX object and then must wait until thread B signals that thread A may continue by calling `Release()` — `Acquire()` and `Release()` act as though they were `Wait()` and `Signal()` functions respectively. However, this usage is unnatural. For it to work correctly, thread B must initially hold the mutex or else thread A will not wait — furthermore, ownership of the mutex is transferred to thread A and so the code cannot be repeated without somehow allowing thread B to reacquire the mutex. These problems are avoided by using an event since threads do not take possession of an event as they do a mutex:

thread A	**thread B**
.	.
`event.Wait();`	.
.	`event.Signal();`
.	.

Here thread A will block in the `Wait()` call until thread B calls `Signal()` — as with threads blocked whilst trying to acquire a mutex, thread A enters its 'Sleeping' state and is then said to be 'sleeping on the event'. In contrast to the mutex version, thread B can call `Signal()` without making a prior call to `Wait()` and when thread A completes its `Wait()` call this does not prevent thread B from calling `Signal()` if the code is repeated — neither thread A nor thread B ever own the event. As noted in section 1.3 an important feature of an event is that it contains a kind of built-in memory — the event can remember if it has been signalled by changing its internal state from 'non-signalled' to 'signalled'. Consequently, the exact time ordering of the `Wait()` and `Signal()` calls made by threads A and B is not important — in particular, if thread A calls `Wait()` after thread B has called `Signal()` then the event is already in the signalled state and so thread A continues immediately.

4.2 The EVENT Class

The EVENT class encapsulates the functionality of an event as supported by the operating system in order to hide the variations which occur between different implementations:

```
class EVENT {
public:
  EVENT(int = TRUE);
  ~EVENT(void);
  void Signal(void);
  void Wait(void);
  void Reset(void);
  int Test(void);
    ...
};
```

The constructor takes a single boolean parameter to indicate whether the event is 'automatic' or 'manual' — by default an automatic event is created. The difference in the two types of event is how the Wait() function affects the internal state of the event — the following figure illustrates the point:

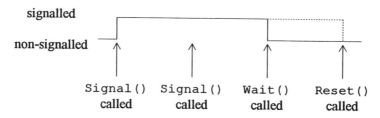

As described in the previous section the first call to Signal() moves the event to the signalled state — subsequent calls to Signal() simply leave the event signalled. For an automatic event the next successful call to Wait() resets the state to non-signalled (full line) whereas for a manual event the Wait() function leaves the state alone (dashed line) — to reset the state of a manual event the Reset() function must be invoked explicitly. Finally, the EVENT class provides a non-blocking Test() function which returns a boolean value to indicate whether or not the event is in the signalled state — for an automatic event in the signalled state the function also resets the state to non-signalled. The Test() function should be treated with care since the return value represents the state of the event as it was when the Test() function examined it — the state may well have changed in the meantime.

The type of event determines how many calls to Wait() can be unblocked by a single call to Signal(). If a lone thread repeatedly calls Wait() for an automatic event then, since the event state is automatically reset each time, there must be a matching series of Signal() calls that keep releasing the thread. Similarly if several threads are currently sleeping on the same automatic event then each signal will cause just one thread to return from Wait() — the first Wait() call to complete resets the state and so all the other threads continue to block. Conversely, for a manual event each invocation of Signal() can allow many successful Wait() calls by one or more threads — the event remains signalled until Reset() is called.

4.3 Using Events

An event can be used for many of the same purposes as a mutex:

— inter-thread communication
— state transitions
— atomic operations

The first two uses reflect different facets of the same technique and rely on the fact that an event can be considered as providing a mutex protected data block

containing the internal state of the event as the only variable. For example, the
LOOPY class of section 3.7 can be rewritten using an event to perform inter-thread
communication by making a state transition:

```
void LOOPY::Quit(void) {
  Event.Signal();
}
```

The EVENT class Signal() and Reset() functions essentially implement state
transitions that always move to signalled and non-signalled states respectively.
With a manual event the current state can be examined non-destructively using
Test() — in the LOOPY class example the state of the event is tested within
Run() to determine when to exit the loop:

```
void* LOOPY::Run(void* param) {
  while (!Event.Test()) {
        ...
  }
  return NULL;
}
```

This version is much cleaner than the previous one because the mutex Acquire()
and Release() calls are effectively implemented within the EVENT class. With
an automatic event the Test() function would reset the state to non-signalled
whenever the loop is exited — however, it may also be necessary to test the event
within the body of the loop so that processing can be aborted as soon as possible
and so the LOOPY class uses a manual event to avoid the automatic reset. The
LOOPY class constructor creates the manual event in the following manner:

```
LOOPY::LOOPY(void) : Event(FALSE) {
      ...
}
```

The : notation allows the invocation of the EVENT class constructor to be specified
explicitly thus preventing the default constructor from providing an automatic
event.

Another example of using events for inter-thread communication is for a master
thread to signal to a slave thread that it should perform some lengthy operation for
the master, hence avoiding delaying the master thread — section 4.5 illustrates a
case where the slave thread runs in the background leaving the master thread to
perform user interaction in the foreground.

The EVENT class Wait() function can be used to implement atomic operations by
blocking other threads until the active thread has completed its processing — when
the atomic operation is complete the active thread releases control by calling
Signal() and, assuming an automatic event, this allows the next thread in the
series to run its atomic operation. For example, a thread may be started and then

held up on an event whilst another thread continues the rest of its initialization procedure without interference — once the atomic operation is complete the new thread is signalled to start running. A variation on this theme is to have a pair of threads alternately hold up the other:

thread A	thread B

```
                  .                            .
                                      start_A->Signal();
    while (...) {                     while (...) {
      start_A->Wait();                  start_B->Wait();
                  .                            .
                  .                            .
                  .                            .
      start_B->Signal();               start_A->Signal();
    }                                }
                  .                            .
```

Here thread A is allowed to execute the code within its **while** loop as an atomic operation whilst thread B is held up on the `start_B` event, then thread B runs whilst thread A is held up. The cycle repeats until eventually each **while** loop detects a terminating condition and processing will cease. The BUFFER class described in the next section illustrates yet another variation of the hold-up technique. For the BUFFER class the reader and writer threads are only held up when the shared data buffer is respectively either empty or full — the flags ReaderWaiting and WriterWaiting are set to tell the other thread when a signal is required.

Sometimes it is useful to pulse an event — the event moves to the signalled state for the duration of the pulse and then returns to the non-signalled state. If there are no threads waiting for the event then the pulse has no effect but if there are waiters then one or more threads should be released — Windows provides a PulseEvent() function which releases one thread for an automatic event and all threads for a manual event. A simple generic implementation of event pulsing using a manual event might be:

```
void Pulse(EVENT* event) {
    event->Signal();
    THREAD::Sleep(10);
    event->Reset();
}
```

However, the resultant behaviour is not well-defined (for example, the same thread could be released multiple times by a single pulse) and the SYNCH class introduced in chapter 5 adopts a better approach.

4.4 The BUFFER Class

The BUFFER class allows data to be buffered between a writer thread and a reader thread — the writer passes data to the WriteData() function and the reader retrieves it by calling ReadData(). The class provides a perfect example of the 'producer-consumer' paradigm since, on the one hand, the writer produces data and the reader consumes it whilst, on the other hand, the reader frees space in the buffer and the writer fills it. The full specification of the BUFFER class is as follows:

```
const int BUFFER_SIZE = 1024;

class BUFFER {
public:
  BUFFER(void);
  ~BUFFER(void);
  void WriteData(char*,int);
  void ReadData(char*,int);
private:
  char Buffer[BUFFER_SIZE];
  int Write;
  int Read;
  int WriterWaiting;
  int ReaderWaiting;
  EVENT Writer;
  EVENT Reader;
  MUTEX Mutex;
};
```

The constructor resets the Write and Read pointers to reference the start of the buffer and the destructor performs no action:

```
BUFFER::BUFFER(void) {
  Write = 0;
  Read = 0;
}

BUFFER::~BUFFER(void) {}
```

The WriteData() function writes data into the buffer — the operation of this function was mostly described in sections 3.7, 3.8 and 3.9 but there are still a couple of points to note. Firstly, when the buffer is full the writer thread sets the WriterWaiting flag and waits for the reader thread to signal the Writer event — the reader thread uses the ReaderWaiting flag and Reader event in a similar manner whenever the buffer is empty. Secondly, the data is actually transferred to (or from) the buffer by calling the memcpy() library routine — if the data in a particular transfer wraps around from the end of the buffer to the start then two calls are necessary. As noted in section 3.7 the data transfer itself can be made without mutex protection — this allows the other thread to continue during a possibly lengthy operation thus increasing the efficiency on a multi-processor system. The full definition of the WriteData() function is as follows:

```
void BUFFER::WriteData(char* data,int length) {
  int space_available;
  int ready = FALSE;
  while (!ready) {
    Mutex.Acquire();
    space_available = Read-Write;
    if (space_available <= 0)
      space_available += BUFFER_SIZE;
    if (length < space_available) {
      Mutex.Release();
      ready = TRUE;
    }
    else {
      WriterWaiting = TRUE;
      Mutex.Release();
      Writer.Wait();
    }
  }
  int space_to_end = (BUFFER_SIZE - Write);
  if (length <= space_to_end)
    memcpy(Buffer+Write,data,length);
  else {
    memcpy(Buffer+Write,data,space_to_end);
    memcpy(Buffer,data+space_to_end,
                      length-space_to_end);
  }
  Mutex.Acquire();
  Write = (Write+length)%BUFFER_SIZE;
  if (ReaderWaiting) {
    ReaderWaiting = FALSE;
    Reader.Signal();
  }
  Mutex.Release();
}
```

The ReadData() function for reading data from the buffer is very similar to the WriteData() function — the reader thread continues in the 'Reading' state until it detects an empty buffer and then it enters the 'Waiting' state setting the ReaderWaiting flag as it does so. Just like the writer thread in the

WriteData() function, the reader thread keeps control of the mutex until the
state transition is complete. The full definition of the ReadData() function is as
follows:

```cpp
void BUFFER::ReadData(char* data,int length) {
  int data_available;
  int ready = FALSE;
  while (!ready) {
    Mutex.Acquire();
    data_available = Write-Read;
    if (data_available < 0)
      data_available += BUFFER_SIZE;
    if (length <= data_available) {
      Mutex.Release();
      ready = TRUE;
    }
    else {
      ReaderWaiting = TRUE;
      Mutex.Release();
      Reader.Wait();
    }
  }
  int data_to_end = (BUFFER_SIZE - Read);
  if (length <= data_to_end)
    memcpy(data,Buffer+Read,length);
  else {
    memcpy(data,Buffer+Read,data_to_end);
    memcpy(data+data_to_end,Buffer,
                     length-data_to_end);
  }
  Mutex.Acquire();
  Read = (Read+length)%BUFFER_SIZE;
  if (WriterWaiting) {
    WriterWaiting = FALSE;
    Writer.Signal();
  }
  Mutex.Release();
}
```

A typical application of the BUFFER class is provided by the TRANSFER class
which embodies a simple communication protocol that prefixes each message with
its length. The TRANSFER class Send() function is defined using the BUFFER
class WriteData() function as follows:

```cpp
void TRANSFER::Send(char* data,int length) {
  Buffer.WriteData((char*)&length,sizeof(int));
  Buffer.WriteData(data,length);
  delete [] data;
}
```

Similarly, the TRANSFER class Receive() function calls the BUFFER class ReadData() function:

```
void TRANSFER::Receive(char** data,int* length) {
    Buffer.ReadData((char*)length,sizeof(int));
    *data = new char[*length];
    Buffer.ReadData(*data,*length);
}
```

A typical data transfer would occur as follows:

```
          writer                              reader
int length = 6;                           .
char* data = new char[length];            .
memcpy(data,"Hello",length);              .
Transfer.Send(data,length);               .
                   .              int length;
                   .              char* data;
                   .              Transfer.Receive(&data,&length);
                   .              // process data
                   .              delete [] data;
```

The writer thread must allocate memory for the message passed into the Send() function — this memory is deallocated internally by the function. Similarly, once the reader thread has finished processing the data returned by the Receive() function, it must release the memory block containing the received message.

4.5 The TIC_TAC_TOE Class

The TIC_TAC_TOE class is designed to play noughts-and-crosses — it maintains a continuous dialogue with its human opponent in the following manner:

```
123
456
789

Enter Move:5
123
406
789

Thinking ...
Thinking ...

123
406
78X

Enter Move:
```

As mentioned in section 4.3 the main() function for the program illustrates how a
master thread can signal to a slave that it should perform some background
computation — here the primary thread acts as master and provides user feedback
by occasionally printing the message Thinking ... whilst the TIC_TAC_TOE
slave thread is deciding upon the machine's next move:

```
int main(int argc, char** argv) {
  int i;
  BOARD Board;
  EVENT Play;
  EVENT Ready;
  TIC_TAC_TOE tic_tac_toe(&Board, &Play, &Ready);
  tic_tac_toe.Start();
  Board.Print();
  while (TRUE) {
    do {
      printf("Enter Move:");
      scanf("%i", &i);
    } while (!Board.Move(i));
    Board.Print();
    if (!Board.GameOver()) {
      Play.Signal();
      do {
        printf("Thinking ...\n");
        THREAD::Sleep(500);
      } while (!Ready.Test());
      Board.Print();
    }
    if (Board.GameOver())
      Board.Clear();
  }
  return 0;
}
```

The main() function firstly creates a BOARD object and two EVENT objects
called Play and Ready — pointers to all three of these objects are passed into the
TIC_TAC_TOE constructor and then the TIC_TAC_TOE slave thread is started.
The BOARD object provides several utility functions for actually playing the game
such as Clear(), Move(), Print() and GameOver() — in particular, the
Move() function checks that the player enters a valid move. The Play event is
used to signal to the slave thread to start calculating the reply to the player's move
and the Ready event can be tested by the master to determine when the calculation
is complete. This is a fairly basic use of multi-threading but it illustrates the
technique — in a more sophisticated application the foreground thread could be

running a graphical user interface and the background thread might spend its idle
time trying to anticipate the player's next move. The TIC_TAC_TOE class has the
following specification:

```
class TIC_TAC_TOE : public THREAD {
public:
  TIC_TAC_TOE(BOARD*,EVENT*,EVENT*);
  ~TIC_TAC_TOE(void);
protected:
  virtual void* Run(void*);
private:
  void Think(int);
  BOARD* Board;
  EVENT* Play;
  EVENT* Ready;
  int Wins;
  int Total;
};
```

The TIC_TAC_TOE class is derived from the THREAD base class and the actions
of the TIC_TAC_TOE slave thread are defined by implementing the secondary
thread function Run() as an endless loop:

```
void* TIC_TAC_TOE::Run(void*) {
  int i,n,wins,total;
  while (TRUE) {
    Play->Wait();
    wins = total = 0;
    for (i=1; (i<=9); i++) {
      Wins = Total = 0;
      Think(i);
      if (Total && ((Wins*total)>=(wins*Total))) {
        wins = Wins;
        total = Total;
        n = i;
      }
    }
    Board->Move(n);
    Ready->Signal();
  }
  return NULL;
}
```

However, to avoid the problem of passing several arguments to the Run() function
when it expects only a single void* parameter, the TIC_TAC_TOE constructor

accepts three pointers which it stores in the object's `Board`, `Play` and `Ready` fields:

```
TIC_TAC_TOE::TIC_TAC_TOE(BOARD* board,
                         EVENT* play,
                         EVENT* ready) {
  Board = board;
  Play = play;
  Ready = ready;
}
```

Since the master thread loops endlessly within the `main()` function, the `TIC_TAC_TOE` destructor will never be invoked and so it performs no processing:

```
TIC_TAC_TOE::~TIC_TAC_TOE(void) {}
```

Meanwhile the slave thread loops endlessly within the `TIC_TAC_TOE` class `Run()` function. On each iteration the slave thread waits on the `Play` event until the master thread signals that the next machine move is required and then the slave examines each possible move in turn by calling the `Think()` function — eventually the slave makes what it considers to be the best move and signals the `Ready` event to inform the master thread. The `Think()` function checks that each move is valid by calling the `BOARD` class `Move()` function and if it is, then `Think()` updates the `TIC_TAC_TOE` class `Total` and `Wins` fields according to the status value set by `Move()` — the `Run()` function picks the best move using the ratio of winning outcomes to the total possible outcomes for each move. The `Think()` function has the following definition:

```
void TIC_TAC_TOE::Think(int i) {
  int n;
  if (Board->Move(i)) {
    switch (Board->Status()) {
    case TIC_TAC_TOE_X_WINS:
      Wins++;
    case TIC_TAC_TOE_DRAW:
      Wins++;
    case TIC_TAC_TOE_O_WINS:
      Total++;
      break;
    case TIC_TAC_TOE_PLAYING:
      for (n=1; (n<=9); n++)
        Think(n);
      break;
    }
    Board->Unmove(i);
  }
}
```

For a win by X (the machine) the `Wins` field is incremented by 2 and for a draw it is incremented by 1 — win, draw or lose the `Total` field is incremented by 1. Of course, the current move may not complete the game and in this case the `Think()` function is called recursively until the game is indeed over — the entire sequence of moves is stored on the stack and as each function call returns the corresponding move is passed to the `Unmove()` function so that the original layout is eventually restored.

The `BOARD` class is the real work-horse of this example and provides all the functionality to actually play a game — however, the class is designed to be used by a single thread and so supplies no thread synchronization internally:

```
class BOARD {
public:
   BOARD(void);
   ~BOARD(void);
   void Clear(void);
   int Move(int);
   void Unmove(int);
   int Status(void);
   int GameOver(void);
   void Print(void);
private:
   void Evaluate(void);
   char Board[9];
   char Player;
   int State;
   static int Lines[8][3];
};
```

The constructor simply calls the `Clear()` function to reset the state of the board whilst the destructor does nothing:

```
BOARD::BOARD(void) {
   Clear();
}

BOARD::~BOARD(void) {}
```

The `Clear()` function empties the board, sets the `State` field to `TIC_TAC_TOE_PLAYING` and lets O (the human) take the first move:

```
void BOARD::Clear(void) {
   for (int i=1; (i<=9); i++)
     Board[i-1] = (char)('0'+i);
   State = TIC_TAC_TOE_PLAYING;
   Player = 'O';
}
```

The `Move()` function firstly verifies that the move is valid and then updates the `State` field by calling `Evaluate()` before finally toggling the `Player` field ready for the next move:

```cpp
int BOARD::Move(int i) {
  i--;
  if (State==TIC_TAC_TOE_PLAYING)
    if ((i>=0) && (i<9))
      if ((Board[i]!='O') && (Board[i]!='X')) {
        Board[i] = Player;
        Evaluate();
        Player = ((Player=='O') ? 'X' : 'O');
        return TRUE;
      }
  return FALSE;
}
```

The `Evaluate()` function looks for lines completely filled by the current player:

```cpp
void BOARD::Evaluate(void) {
  int i, n;
  for (i=0; (i<8); i++) {
    for (n=0; (n<3); n++)
      if (Board[Lines[i][n]-1] != Player)
        break;
    if (n == 3)
      break;
  }
  if (i < 8)
    State = ((Player == 'O') ?
      TIC_TAC_TOE_O_WINS : TIC_TAC_TOE_X_WINS);
  else {
    for (i=0; (i<9); i++)
      if ((Board[i]!='O') && (Board[i]!='X'))
        break;
    if (i == 9)
      State = TIC_TAC_TOE_DRAW;
  }
}
```

The winning lines are stored in the static `Lines` field:

```cpp
int BOARD::Lines[8][3] = {{1,2,3},{4,5,6},{7,8,9},
                          {1,4,7},{2,5,8},{3,6,9},
                          {1,5,9},{3,5,7}};
```

If a complete line is found then the `State` field is updated to either `TIC_TAC_TOE_O_WINS` or `TIC_TAC_TOE_X_WINS` as appropriate. If neither player has won the `Evaluate()` function then checks for a full board so that the

State field can be set to TIC_TAC_TOE_DRAW — otherwise the state is left as
TIC_TAC_TOE_PLAYING. The TIC_TAC_TOE class internal helper function
Think() examines the State field using the BOARD class Status() function:

```
int BOARD::Status(void) {
  return State;
}
```

The BOARD class convenience function GameOver() allows external code to
easily determine when the State field changes from TIC_TAC_TOE_PLAYING:

```
int BOARD::GameOver(void) {
  return (State != TIC_TAC_TOE_PLAYING);
}
```

The Unmove() function reverses the actions of the Move() function — it
restores the Player field to its previous value, resets the State field to
TIC_TAC_TOE_PLAYING and clears the last space on the board to be filled by
an X or an O:

```
void BOARD::Unmove(int i) {
  Player = ((Player=='O') ? 'X' : 'O');
  State = TIC_TAC_TOE_PLAYING;
  Board[i-1] = (char)('0'+i);
}
```

Finally, the BOARD class Print() function prints out the board contents in the
format illustrated at the start of the section:

```
void BOARD::Print(void) {
  for (int i=0;(i<9);i++) {
    if ((i%3)==0)
      printf("\n");
    printf("%c",Board[i]);
  }
  printf("\n\n");
  switch (State) {
  case TIC_TAC_TOE_O_WINS:
    printf("O Wins\n\n");
    break;
  case TIC_TAC_TOE_X_WINS:
    printf("X Wins\n\n");
    break;
  case TIC_TAC_TOE_DRAW:
    printf("Draw\n\n");
    break;
  }
}
```

The Print() function also prints out a message if either player wins or it is a
draw — in this case the board will subsequently be cleared and a new game started.

From one perspective the TIC_TAC_TOE class can be regarded as simply
supplying a secondary thread of execution with the class fields providing a
convenient alternative to global variables for passing data between the various
functions. An alternative view, however, is that the thread run by the
TIC_TAC_TOE object transforms it into an independent entity that is capable of
servicing external requests in an asynchronous manner — C++ objects which use
internal threads like this are termed 'active' objects and they form the subject
matter of chapter 6.

4.6 UNIX Implementation

The POSIX standard for UNIX does not supply any event synchronization
primitives directly but instead defines 'condition variables' — these act very much
like an event but without built-in memory so that a signal is not remembered until
the next pthread_cond_wait() call. Each EVENT object must embed a
pthread_cond_t structure and also a pthread_mutex_t structure since a
condition variable requires the protection of an associated mutex:

```
event.h:

#ifndef _EVENT_HEADER
#define _EVENT_HEADER

#include "unix.h"
#include <pthread.h>

class EVENT {
public:
   EVENT(int = TRUE);
   ~EVENT(void);
   void Signal(void);
   void Wait(void);
   void Reset(void);
   int Test(void);
private:
   pthread_cond_t Event;
   pthread_mutex_t Mutex;
   int Automatic;
   int Active;
};

#endif
```

The EVENT class constructor takes a boolean parameter to specify either an automatic event or a manual event — by default the constructor creates an automatic event:

`event.cxx:`

```
#include "unix.h"
#include <pthread.h>
#include "event.h"

EVENT::EVENT(int automatic) {
  pthread_cond_init(&Event, (pthread_condattr_t*)NULL);
  pthread_mutex_init(&Mutex, (pthread_mutexattr_t*)NULL);
  Automatic = automatic;
  Active = FALSE;
}
```

The constructor initializes the EVENT object's condition variable and mutex by calling the functions `pthread_cond_init()` and `pthread_mutex_init()` — the NULL parameters indicate that default attributes are required. The Active field is set to FALSE to place the event initially in its non-signalled state — the EVENT object uses this field to complement its condition variable with the necessary built-in memory facility and so implement the functionality of an event. The EVENT class destructor releases the operating system resources by calling the `pthread_cond_destroy()` and `pthread_mutex_destroy()` functions:

```
EVENT::~EVENT(void) {
  pthread_cond_destroy(&Event);
  pthread_mutex_destroy(&Mutex);
}
```

The EVENT class Signal() function works by setting the Active field to TRUE (thus moving the event to the signalled state) and then calling either `pthread_cond_signal()` or `pthread_cond_broadcast()` dependent on whether the event is automatic or manual:

```
void EVENT::Signal(void) {
  pthread_mutex_lock(&Mutex);
  Active = TRUE;
  if (Automatic)
    pthread_cond_signal(&Event);
  else
    pthread_cond_broadcast(&Event);
  pthread_mutex_unlock(&Mutex);
}
```

Both of the `pthread_cond_signal()` and `pthread_cond_broadcast()` functions take a condition variable as a parameter and release threads currently waiting on this condition variable — if there are no waiting threads then the signal is not remembered by the condition variable but by the `Active` field instead. The difference between the two functions `pthread_cond_signal()` and `pthread_cond_broadcast()` is that the former guarantees to release only a single waiting thread whilst the latter will release all of them — for an automatic event only one thread will exit from its `Wait()` call so there is no need to awaken more than one thread but for a manual event it is possible that all the threads may be able to complete their `Wait()` calls before the event is reset. A thread calling `Wait()` checks the `Active` field for a remembered signal before waiting on the condition variable in the `pthread_cond_wait()` function:

```
void EVENT::Wait(void) {
  pthread_mutex_lock(&Mutex);
  while (!Active)
    pthread_cond_wait(&Event,&Mutex);
  if (Automatic)
    Active = FALSE;
  pthread_mutex_unlock(&Mutex);
}
```

When `Signal()` sets the event state to signalled and then signals the condition variable, the `pthread_cond_wait()` function releases its waiting threads and they loop to re-examine the `Active` field — the `pthread_cond_wait()` function performs an internal call to `pthread_mutex_unlock()` when it starts to wait and a matching call to `pthread_mutex_lock()` when the thread is released and so any waiters are released serially. For an automatic event the first thread released exits the loop and resets the state to non-signalled — for a manual event the state is not reset automatically and possibly all the waiting threads can exit the **while** loop. As a technical point there is a low probability that `pthread_cond_wait()` will return even without a signal — however, the check on the `Active` field prevents the loop from terminating prematurely in this case. Also in the `Signal()` function the call to `pthread_cond_signal()` or `pthread_cond_broadcast()` should be bracketed within the mutex block for reliable operation — the `pthread_cond_wait()` function must set a `Waiting` flag before releasing its hold on the mutex (as do the reader and writer threads from the `BUFFER` class of section 4.4) and that ought to happen before a signal is allowed to occur. Indeed this is the reason why the `pthread_cond_wait()` function releases the mutex internally — if the mutex were to be released before the `Waiting` flag is set then an intervening signal would be lost leaving the waiting thread blocked indefinitely. Fortunately, the `Reset()` function is a straightforward example of a mutex block used to perform a state transition:

```
void EVENT::Reset(void) {
  pthread_mutex_lock(&Mutex);
  Active = FALSE;
  pthread_mutex_unlock(&Mutex);
}
```

The EVENT class `Test()` function examines the current state of the event and atomically resets the event to the non-signalled state if it is an automatic event:

```
int EVENT::Test(void) {
  pthread_mutex_lock(&Mutex);
  int active = Active;
  if (Active && Automatic)
    Active = FALSE;
  pthread_mutex_unlock(&Mutex);
  return active;
}
```

Here the local variable `active` is used to take a snapshot of the event state from the shared `Active` field — the recorded value is returned by the `Test()` function and the actual state of the event may well change in the meantime.

4.7 Windows Implementation

Since Windows does indeed provide an event synchronization primitive, the implementation of the EVENT class is much easier than under UNIX — each EVENT object simply creates a Windows event and holds a handle to reference this event. The full specification for the EVENT class is as follows:

```
event.h:

#ifndef _EVENT_HEADER
#define _EVENT_HEADER

#include <windows.h>

class EVENT {
public:
  EVENT(int = TRUE);
  ~EVENT(void);
  void Signal(void);
  void Wait(void);
  void Reset(void);
  int Test(void);
private:
  HANDLE Event;
};

#endif
```

The Windows event is created in the EVENT class constructor and released in the destructor:

```
event.cxx:

#include <windows.h>
#include "event.h"

EVENT::EVENT(int automatic) {
  Event = CreateEvent(NULL,!automatic,FALSE,NULL);
}

EVENT::~EVENT(void) {
  CloseHandle(Event);
}
```

An automatic or manual event is specified by the second parameter to CreateEvent() whilst the third parameter indicates that the event should initially be in the non-signalled state — the remaining two parameters to this function are passed NULL values as discussed in section 3.11. The EVENT class Signal() and Reset() functions change the state of the event by calling the appropriate operating system functions:

```
void EVENT::Signal(void) {
  SetEvent(Event);
}

void EVENT::Reset(void) {
  ResetEvent(Event);
}
```

The EVENT class Wait() and Test() functions are implemented in a similar manner to the MUTEX class Acquire() and Acquired() functions by calling the generic Windows function WaitForSingleObject() with the Event handle as a parameter:

```
void EVENT::Wait(void) {
  WaitForSingleObject(Event,INFINITE);
}

int EVENT::Test(void) {
  return (WaitForSingleObject(Event,0)!=WAIT_TIMEOUT);
}
```

As with the MUTEX class the blocking and non-blocking calls specify infinite and zero timeout values respectively. For an automatic event the state is atomically reset to non-signalled by WaitForSingleObject() whereas the state of a manual event is unaffected — this behaviour correctly implements the functionality of the EVENT class directly.

4.8 Summary

Whereas a mutex arbitrates amongst a number of competing threads, an event permits a collection of cooperating threads to coordinate their activities. An event provides a two-handed communications mechanism which allows one thread to signal that something has happened and another thread to wait for this signal — unlike mutexes there is no concept of owning an event so any threads are free to signal or wait as required. The EVENT class embodies the functionality of an event in a manner independent of the underlying operating system — specific implementations of the class for UNIX and Windows have been described. Since Windows supports the event synchronization primitive directly the implementation of the EVENT class is straightforward but under the POSIX standard for UNIX only 'condition variables' are available and this slightly complicates the design. The EVENT class provides Signal() and Wait() functions to perform the basic event operations of signalling and waiting — the class also defines Reset() and Test() functions. The EVENT class Signal() function moves the event to its 'signalled' state thereby releasing any threads blocked in Wait() — if there are currently no waiters then the event contains built-in memory to remember the signal until a later Wait() call. There are two types of event (automatic or manual) which differ in the functionality of Wait() — an automatic event automatically resets the event state to 'non-signalled' upon the successful completion of a Wait() call whereas a manual event does not. The EVENT class Reset() function is provided to reset the state of a manual event. The difference in operation of Wait() for automatic and manual events influences the number of threads which each Signal() call can release — for an automatic event a single thread will be released exactly once but for a manual event it is possible for many threads to be released multiple times before the event is reset. Finally, the EVENT class Test() function enables external code to take a snapshot of the internal state of the event without risk of blocking — with an automatic event the Test() function also atomically resets the event to the non-signalled state if it is currently signalled. An EVENT object can be applied in many of the same ways as a MUTEX object — however, it is particularly useful in holding up the execution of a thread until the program is ready for it to continue without the thread having to waste processor cycles in polling the value of some flag. The classic example of this usage is the 'producer-consumer' paradigm where a producer thread produces some quantity before signalling an event whilst a consumer thread waits on the event and then consumes the quantity — often the cycle is repeated as it is in the BUFFER class which buffers data between a pair of writer and reader threads. The TIC_TAC_TOE class illustrates another application of an event — here a master thread signals to a slave thread that it should perform some lengthy computation in the background leaving the master thread responsive to user input in the foreground.

5. Semaphores

All thread synchronization can be performed using the synchronization primitives mutexes and events — a mutex arbitrates amongst a collection of competing threads whilst an event allows cooperating threads to coordinate their interactions. Nonetheless, a semaphore is a useful generalization of an event which contains a built-in counter — the semaphore also incorporates its own mutex protection for the counter to ensure that it is not corrupted if several threads attempt to modify its value simultaneously. A semaphore provides `Signal()` and `Wait()` functions which act in a similar manner to the corresponding functions for an event — however, whereas the event versions change the event state to signalled or non-signalled, the semaphore `Signal()` function increments the semaphore count and the `Wait()` function decrements it, only blocking if the value reaches zero. The functionality supported by a semaphore is representative of a more general pattern of thread synchronization (which incidentally also describes the operation of an event) — this chapter introduces the `SYNCH` base class that is designed to encapsulate this generic method of synchronization and from which the `SEMAPHORE` class may be derived. The chapter also provides examples of three semaphore applications — the `POOL` class shows how a semaphore can monitor the number of resources that are currently available from a pool, the `PIPELINE` class expands on the producer-consumer paradigm from the previous chapter with the semaphore counting the number of commodities in transit from producer to consumer, and finally the `ARBITRATOR` class illustrates the use of a semaphore in allowing multiple 'reader' threads to reliably examine some resource whilst a single 'writer' thread periodically updates its state. The main topics covered here include:

— generic synchronization patterns
— context parameters
— the `SYNCH` class
— the `SEMAPHORE` class
— the `POOL` class
— transferring information between threads
— the `PIPELINE` class
— the `ARBITRATOR` class
— implementation details for UNIX and Windows

The chapter also discusses some of the pitfalls that can ensnare the unwary multi-threaded programmer and provides an introduction to the thought processes required to eventually achieve a successful design.

5.1 Synchronization Patterns

The BUFFER class from section 4.4 defines the functions WriteData() and
ReadData() to enable a pair of writer and reader threads to transfer data via a
buffer. The BUFFER class WriteData() function has the following form:

```
void WriteData(...) {
  // wait for enough space
  // write data to buffer
  // signal data available
}
```

Similarly, the BUFFER class ReadData() function has the following form:

```
void ReadData(...) {
  // wait for enough data
  // read data from buffer
  // signal space available
}
```

The actual data transfer to and from the buffer is straightforward and requires no
thread synchronization — however, the code sections which perform 'wait' and
'signal' operations involve quite tricky management of several synchronization
primitives. The code in WriteData() which waits for buffer space and the code
in ReadData() which waits for fresh data could both be cast into the following
form:

```
void Wait(void) {
  int status;
  do {
    Mutex.Acquire();
    status = Status();
    Mutex.Release();
    if (status == WAIT)
      Event.Wait();
  } while (status == WAIT);
}
```

The Status() function is used to particularize the code to a specific situation
— for the writer thread it tests for sufficient buffer space and sets the
WriterWaiting flag if this is not available whilst for the reader thread the
Status() function checks to see if enough data has arrived and if not then
it sets the ReaderWaiting flag. The code in WriteData() and ReadData()

which signals that more data has been sent or received can similarly be transformed into a more general form:

```
void Signal(void) {
  Mutex.Acquire();
  if (Update())
    Event.Signal();
  Mutex.Release();
}
```

For the BUFFER class, depending on whether the writer or reader thread is involved, the Update() function either updates the Write pointer and checks the ReaderWaiting flag or alternatively updates the Read pointer and checks the WriterWaiting flag — the event is only signalled if the appropriate flag has been set and the Update() function consequently returns TRUE.

In fact the basic synchronization patterns defined by the generic Signal() and Wait() functions are quite widely applicable and so it makes sense to package them within a C++ class — indeed this is the topic of the following section. Furthermore, this approach enforces the re-use of a reliable design rather than requiring each application to devise its own potentially flawed variation — even minor deviations in form must be considered very carefully as the following modification illustrates:

```
void Wait(void) {
  int status;
  do {
    Mutex.Acquire();
    status = Status();
    Mutex.Release();
    if (status == WAIT)
      Block();
  } while (status == WAIT);
}
```

This version of Wait() implements a Waiter flag directly — instead of just blocking on an event, the Block() function is called to first set the Waiter flag thus indicating that a signal is required:

```
void Block(void) {
  Mutex.Acquire();
  Waiter = TRUE;
  Mutex.Release();
  Event.Wait();
}
```

The `Signal()` function checks the `Waiter` flag to decide whether or not to signal:

```
void Signal(void) {
  Mutex.Acquire();
  Update();
  if (Waiter) {
    Waiter = FALSE;
    Event.Signal();
  }
  Mutex.Release();
}
```

This appears to be a fairly innocuous change but now it is possible for threads to be blocked in `Wait()` indefinitely when they should have been released by a `Signal()` call — indeed this hazard was highlighted in section 3.8 when discussing the BUFFER class. The problem occurs if the `Status()` function returns WAIT then the state is updated by `Update()` but the `Waiter` flag is still FALSE because it has not yet been set by `Block()` and so the signal is lost leaving the waiting thread to hang. The problem, of course, is that the mutex is released (then reacquired) before the transition to the waiting state is complete — the code will function correctly if the `Mutex` object `Acquire()` call at the start of `Block()` is removed and the `Wait()` function is modified as follows:

```
void Wait(void) {
  int status;
  do {
    Mutex.Acquire();
    status = Status();
    if (status == WAIT)
      Block();
    else
      Mutex.Release();
  } while (status == WAIT);
}
```

The changes ensure that the state transition is packaged within a single mutex block.

5.2 The SYNCH Class

The SYNCH class embodies the essential features of the synchronization patterns described in the previous section — it will act as a base class for various derived classes such as the SEMAPHORE class of the following section, the RECURSIVE_MUTEX_SYNCH class of section 8.3 and the MULTI_EVENT class of section 9.6.

The SYNCH class has the following specification:

```
class SYNCH {
public:
  SYNCH(void);
  virtual ~SYNCH(void);
  int Wait(void* = NULL);
  void Signal(void* = NULL);
  void Broadcast(void* = NULL);
protected:
  virtual int Status(void*);
  virtual int Update(void*);
    ...
};
```

As well as the expected Wait() and Signal() functions there is also a
Broadcast() function — whereas the Signal() function guarantees to release
at least one thread waiting in Wait() so that it can re-evaluate the current state
with a fresh call to Status(), the Broadcast() function will release all such
waiting threads although, of course, some of them might not exit the Wait()
function. An important point to note is that the SYNCH class Signal() and
Broadcast() functions will only release threads that are currently waiting and
there is no concept of remembering a signal or broadcast — the paradigm for
waiting and signalling supported by the SYNCH class is consequently very similar
to that defined for UNIX condition variables. The logic behind this design is that
classes derived from the SYNCH class will provide their own state variables to
perform the memory function present in the EVENT class — for example, the
SEMAPHORE class described in the following section records the number of unused
signals in an integer Count field.

All three of the SYNCH class functions Wait(), Signal() and Broadcast()
take a 'context' parameter which defaults to NULL — the Wait() function
passes its parameter along to the Status() function whilst Signal() and
Broadcast() pass their parameter along to Update(). The context parameter
enables different threads to perform different synchronization activities in much the
same way that the initialization parameter to the THREAD class Start() function
allows different threads sharing the same Run() function to specialize their
behaviours — for example, the MULTI_EVENT class uses the context parameter to
the Wait() function to indicate which one of several events to wait for. An
alternative approach might be to pass context information using class fields but as
these are shared by different threads mutex protection would be required — the
technique is suitable for the Signal() and Broadcast() functions but not for
Wait() which could block indefinitely. Yet another possibility (which would work
with all three functions) is to supply the necessary context using the thread-specific
storage provided by a 'key' — section 7.2 illustrates an application of this
mechanism.

The SYNCH class Status() and Update() functions are virtual and must be overridden in classes derived from the SYNCH base class to specify the individual functionality of the derived class. These two functions operate upon the collection of state variables that the class uses to implement its synchronization capabilities — for example, the current state of each SEMAPHORE object is defined by its Count field. The Update() function should update the state variables and return a boolean value indicating whether or not to send a signal to release any threads waiting in Wait() — for example, as discussed in the previous section, it may be desirable only to signal whenever another thread has already explicitly requested this action by setting its Waiter flag. The Status() function examines the state variables to determine whether a thread must block within the Wait() function or whether it can continue immediately — the Status() function has the option of returning one of the following three values:

```
const int SYNCH_FAIL = 0;
const int SYNCH_OKAY = 1;
const int SYNCH_WAIT = 2;
```

The Status() function returns SYNCH_WAIT if the calling thread must wait whilst the other two return values allow the thread to proceed — the SYNCH_OKAY value indicates that the thread has successfully waited for some synchronization condition to be achieved (or that no wait is necessary) whilst the SYNCH_FAIL value means that the Wait() call should terminate unsuccessfully. The SYNCH_OKAY and SYNCH_FAIL values are respectively converted to TRUE and FALSE return values from the Wait() function — the non-blocking RECURSIVE_MUTEX class Acquired() function of section 8.3, for example, uses this facility to report whether or not the mutex was successfully acquired. In addition to examining the current state, the Status() function may also atomically update the state variables — the EVENT class Wait() function performs a similar action whenever it resets the state of the event to non-signalled.

5.3 The SEMAPHORE Class

The SEMAPHORE class provides the first concrete example of deriving a synchronization class from the SYNCH base class. The SEMAPHORE class resembles the EVENT class but whereas the latter permits an EVENT object to assume one of two states (signalled or non-signalled) the former incorporates a Count field capable of holding the values 0, 1, 2, ... corresponding to many different possible states for each SEMAPHORE object — the basic operation of the SEMAPHORE class is for the Signal() function to increment the semaphore count whilst the Wait() function decrements it.

The full specification of the SEMAPHORE class is as follows:

```
semaphore.h:

#ifndef _SEMAPHORE_HEADER
#define _SEMAPHORE_HEADER

#include "synch.h"

class SEMAPHORE : public SYNCH {
public:
  SEMAPHORE(int = 0);
  ~SEMAPHORE(void);
  int Test(void);
protected:
  virtual int Status(void*);
  virtual int Update(void*);
private:
  int Count;
};

#endif
```

In addition to the functions specified explicitly the SEMAPHORE class inherits the Wait(), Signal() and Broadcast() functions from the SYNCH class — however, the Broadcast() function is actually superfluous. The base class functions take **void*** parameters but external code using a SEMAPHORE object must not supply these explicitly and instead accept the default NULL values — similarly, the Wait() function returns a boolean value but this will always be TRUE for the SEMAPHORE class and so it should be ignored by external code. The SEMAPHORE class can consequently be regarded as providing the somewhat cleaner interface:

```
class SEMAPHORE {
public:
  void Signal(void);
  void Wait(void);
  int Test(void);
      ...
};
```

Indeed C++ would allow the SEMAPHORE class to hide the base class functions and enforce the new interface but this approach is not adopted here.

The SEMAPHORE class constructor sets the Count field to some initial value 0, 1, 2, ... and the destructor does nothing:

```
semaphore.cxx:

#include "synch.h"
#include "semaphore.h"

SEMAPHORE::SEMAPHORE(int count) {
  Count = (count>=0 ? count : 0);
}

SEMAPHORE::~SEMAPHORE(void) {}
```

The Signal() function increments the Count field and always sends a signal to any waiting thread since Update() always returns TRUE:

```
int SEMAPHORE::Update(void*) {
  return ++Count;
}
```

The Wait() function waits until the Count value is non-zero and then decrements the semaphore count atomically before returning — the Test() function acts as a non-blocking alternative to Wait() returning FALSE whenever Wait() would block on a zero count. The functionality of both Wait() and Test() is implemented by the SEMAPHORE class Status() function:

```
int SEMAPHORE::Status(void* non_blocking) {
  int status = SYNCH_WAIT;
  if (Count) {
    Count--;
    status = SYNCH_OKAY;
  }
  else if (non_blocking)
    status = SYNCH_FAIL;
  return status;
}
```

For Wait() the non_blocking context parameter defaults to NULL whereas for Test() this parameter is explicitly set to a non-NULL value before Wait() is called internally:

```
int SEMAPHORE::Test(void) {
  int non_blocking;
  return Wait(&non_blocking);
}
```

Hence, within a Wait() call the Status() function will return SYNCH_WAIT until the semaphore count becomes non-zero and then returns SYNCH_OKAY to release the waiting thread — however, if the count is initially zero when `Test()` is invoked then `Status()` will immediately return the additional value `SYNCH_FAIL`.

5.4 The `POOL` Class

This section and the following two illustrate three uses for the counter embedded within a `SEMAPHORE` object — in this section the counter is used to track the number of essentially identical resources that are currently available from a pool. In particular, the `MEMORY_POOL` class manages a pool of memory blocks which can be allocated and deallocated by various threads as required — for example:

```
MEMORY_POOL pool(100);
    ...
char* block = (char*)pool.Allocate();
block[0] = 'x';
pool.Deallocate(block);
```

Here a `MEMORY_POOL` object is created that will be shared by the various threads, then one thread allocates a block from the pool, uses the memory, and finally deallocates the block. The `MEMORY_POOL` class is actually derived from the `POOL` base class which allows a generic pool of resources to be managed — the full specification for the `POOL` class is as follows:

```
class POOL {
public:
    POOL(int);
    virtual ~POOL(void);
    void* Allocate(void);
    void Deallocate(void*);
protected:
    void* Resources[POOL_MAX_RESOURCES];
private:
    int Free[POOL_MAX_RESOURCES];
    int ResourceCount;
    SEMAPHORE Semaphore;
    MUTEX Mutex;
};
```

Each `POOL` object contains a `Resources` array holding pointers that reference the actual resources — the `Free` array indicates whether or not the various resources are currently allocated. For simplicity of design the maximum number of resources available from each `POOL` object is fixed by the following constant:

```
const int POOL_MAX_RESOURCES = 100;
```

The constructor accepts a parameter that allows the number of managed resources to be reduced from the maximum value — the constructor marks the required number of resources as initially free and increments the embedded SEMAPHORE object's counter by calling its Signal() function once for each resource:

```
POOL::POOL(int resource_count) {
  if (resource_count>0 &&
        resource_count<=POOL_MAX_RESOURCES)
    ResourceCount = resource_count;
  else
    ResourceCount = POOL_MAX_RESOURCES;
  for (int i=0; (i<ResourceCount); i++) {
    Resources[i] = NULL;
    Free[i] = TRUE;
    Semaphore.Signal();
  }
}
```

The pointers in the Resources array are set to NULL by the POOL class constructor — they must be properly initialized within the constructor of each derived class. However, the base class destructor takes care of finally releasing the resources as it iterates through the Resources array:

```
POOL::~POOL(void) {
  for (int i=0; (i<ResourceCount); i++)
    delete Resources[i];
}
```

Note that neither the constructor nor the destructor require mutex protection since it is assumed that only a single thread will be involved in creating or destroying the POOL object — conversely, mutex protection is definitely required in the Allocate() and Deallocate() functions to avoid corruption of the internal data structures. The Allocate() function waits on the POOL object's semaphore until a non-zero count indicates that there is at least one free resource — the function then scans the Free array looking for the first resource currently marked as free and allocates it to the requesting thread:

```
void* POOL::Allocate(void) {
  int i;
  Semaphore.Wait();
  Mutex.Acquire();
  for (i=0; (i<ResourceCount); i++)
    if (Free[i])
      break;
  Free[i] = FALSE;
  Mutex.Release();
  return Resources[i];
}
```

Note that the semaphore count is automatically decremented by the Wait() function so it is impossible for a thread to be searching for a free resource and find that other threads have already allocated them all — the Wait() function stakes a claim to a free resource which cannot be stolen. The Deallocate() function similarly scans through the Resources array under mutex protection — once it locates the correct pointer the resource can be marked as free and the semaphore count incremented:

```
void POOL::Deallocate(void* resource) {
  int i;
  Mutex.Acquire();
  for (i=0; (i<ResourceCount); i++)
    if (resource == Resources[i])
      break;
  if (i < ResourceCount) {
    Free[i] = TRUE;
    Semaphore.Signal();
  }
  Mutex.Release();
}
```

The derived MEMORY_POOL class has the following specification:

```
class MEMORY_POOL : public POOL {
public:
  MEMORY_POOL(int);
  virtual ~MEMORY_POOL(void);
};
```

The MEMORY_POOL constructor must create the pool of memory blocks for the MEMORY_POOL object but the destructor need perform no processing:

```
MEMORY_POOL::MEMORY_POOL(int block_count)
      : POOL(block_count) {
  for (int i=0; (i<block_count); i++)
    Resources[i] = new BLOCK;
}

MEMORY_POOL::~MEMORY_POOL(void) {}
```

The memory blocks are actually allocated as BLOCK objects each containing an array of bytes:

```
const int MEMORY_POOL_BLOCK_SIZE = 1024;

struct BLOCK {
  char Data[MEMORY_POOL_BLOCK_SIZE];
};
```

The memory blocks cannot simply be allocated directly as character arrays of length MEMORY_POOL_BLOCK_SIZE because the **delete** operator in the POOL class destructor expects only a single object to delete and not an array — the C++ language has the irritating peculiarity that deletion of arrays requires the [] marker after the **delete** keyword. Fortunately, when the MEMORY_POOL class Allocate() function returns a **void*** pointer to a freshly allocated BLOCK object, this pointer can be converted to **char*** type using a simple C++ type casting operation. The MEMORY_POOL class Allocate() function will be held up indefinitely whenever there are no memory blocks remaining in the pool — this action contrasts with that of the C++ **new** operator which simply returns a NULL pointer whenever its memory resources are exhausted. In some circumstances the MEMORY_POOL class behaviour may be advantageous since the Allocate() function will always succeed eventually (assuming, of course, that the **new** operations in the constructor properly initialize the MEMORY_POOL object) but it does open up the possibility of 'deadlock' whereby one or more threads become blocked forever. The general question of deadlock is discussed in much more detail in chapter 8 whilst chapter 10 describes the derivation of another resource pool class where the deadlock issue is not relevant.

5.5 The PIPELINE Class

The BUFFER class described in section 4.4 provides one method of transferring data from one thread to another — the next chapter shows how to extend this example to allow multiple writer threads to communicate with a single reader thread. An alternative approach to buffering information between threads is to pass messages via a pipeline from writers to readers — the PIPELINE class introduced in this section embodies this technique. The PIPELINE class uses a SEMAPHORE object to keep a count of the number of items currently in the pipeline — the semaphore also allows reader threads to block on it whenever the pipeline is empty. The items passing through the pipeline will each be packaged within an ITEM object and so a description of the ITEM class is a useful preliminary to the implementation of the PIPELINE class itself:

```
class ITEM {
public:
    ITEM(void*);
    ~ITEM(void);
    void Insert(ITEM*);
    void Append(ITEM*);
    void Remove(void);
    ITEM* GetNext(void);
    ITEM* GetPrevious(void);
    void* GetData(void);
private:
    ITEM* Next;
    ITEM* Previous;
    void* Data;
};
```

The data for an item is stored by passing a **void*** pointer parameter to the ITEM constructor which then assigns it to the Data field — the constructor also initializes the Next and Previous fields whilst the destructor performs no action:

```
ITEM::ITEM(void* data) {
  Data = data;
  Next = Previous = this;
}

ITEM::~ITEM(void) {}
```

The data can be obtained by calling the ITEM class GetData() function:

```
void* ITEM::GetData(void) {
  return Data;
}
```

The Next and Previous fields are used to connect a series of ITEM objects into a doubly-linked circular list as follows:

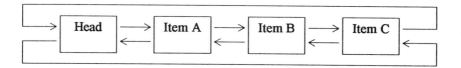

The Next and Previous pointers allow the list to be traversed in either direction and they can be obtained by external code using the GetNext() and GetPrevious() functions:

```
ITEM* ITEM::GetNext(void) {
  return Next;
}

ITEM* ITEM::GetPrevious(void) {
  return Previous;
}
```

The Insert() function enables a new ITEM object to be inserted into the list just before the item passed in as a parameter:

```
void ITEM::Insert(ITEM* item) {
  Next = item;
  Previous = item->Previous;
  Next->Previous = this;
  Previous->Next = this;
}
```

The following figure illustrates the operation of the `Insert()` function when inserting item B before item C:

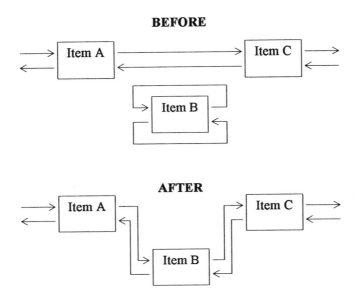

BEFORE

AFTER

If an item is inserted before the `Head` item at the start of the list, this effectively positions the new item at the tail of the list — indeed this is the method used by the `PIPELINE` class to add items to the end of the pipeline. The `ITEM` class also defines an `Append()` function that inserts a new `ITEM` object into the list immediately after the item specified as a parameter:

```
void ITEM::Append(ITEM* item) {
   Previous = item;
   Next = item->Next;
   Previous->Next = this;
   Next->Previous = this;
}
```

The `Append()` function complements the `Insert()` function (exchanging the roles of `Next` and `Previous` pointers) but it is not actually used by the `PIPELINE` class.

The `ITEM` class `Remove()` function removes an item from the list by reversing the actions needed to insert it:

```
void ITEM::Remove(void) {
   Next->Previous = Previous;
   Previous->Next = Next;
   Next = Previous = this;
}
```

The PIPELINE class builds on the functionality of the ITEM class by using a mutex to protect the list data structure from corruption when there are multiple interacting threads and also by adding a semaphore to count the number of items currently in the list — the specification for the PIPELINE class is as follows:

```
class PIPELINE {
public:
    PIPELINE(void);
    ~PIPELINE(void);
    void Put(void*);
    void* Get(void);
private:
    SEMAPHORE Semaphore;
    MUTEX Mutex;
    ITEM* Head;
};
```

The PIPELINE class constructor creates an internal ITEM object to act as the head of the list:

```
PIPELINE::PIPELINE(void) {
    Head = new ITEM(NULL);
}
```

The Head item is destroyed by the PIPELINE class destructor which also deletes any other items remaining in the list and the data that they contain:

```
PIPELINE::~PIPELINE(void) {
    ITEM* item;
    while ((item = Head->GetNext()) != Head) {
        item->Remove();
        delete item->GetData();
        delete item;
    }
    delete Head;
}
```

The Head item simplifies the Put() and Get() functions by ensuring that the list is never empty — the Put() function has the following definition:

```
void PIPELINE::Put(void* data) {
    Mutex.Acquire();
    ITEM* item = new ITEM(data);
    item->Insert(Head);
    Mutex.Release();
    Semaphore.Signal();
}
```

The data passed to the Put() function is packaged into an ITEM object and this is then inserted at the tail of the list — the data enters the end of the pipeline and any other data already in the pipeline will be received first. The counter within the embedded `Semaphore` object is incremented to signal to some thread that it can retrieve the data by calling the `PIPELINE` class `Get()` function:

```
void* PIPELINE::Get(void) {
  Semaphore.Wait();
  Mutex.Acquire();
  ITEM* item = Head->GetNext();
  void* data = item->GetData();
  item->Remove();
  delete item;
  Mutex.Release();
  return data;
}
```

When `Get()` is invoked the thread waits on the `Semaphore` object until some data is available and then it takes the first item from the pipeline — the `ITEM` object immediately following the `Head` item is removed from the list and the data it contains is extracted. As noted in the previous section, the semaphore automatically decrements its internal counter whenever the `Wait()` call succeeds and this ensures that there will definitely be at least one item still available by the time the thread manages to acquire the mutex. Conversely, suppose that the semaphore were to be replaced with a manual event and a counter decremented as soon as the mutex is acquired:

```
void* PIPELINE::Get(void) {
  Event.Wait();
  Mutex.Acquire();
  if (--Counter == 0)
    Event.Reset();
        ...
  Mutex.Release();
  return data;
}
```

In this case too many threads may pass the `Wait()` call before the event is reset by an empty pipeline — of course, an automatic event plus a counter could be substituted successfully for the semaphore:

```
void* PIPELINE::Get(void) {
  Event.Wait();
  Mutex.Acquire();
  if (--Counter)
    Event.Signal();
        ...
  Mutex.Release();
  return data;
}
```

Indeed, as noted at the start of the chapter, thread synchronization without semaphores is possible but they often provide the most convenient solution to a problem. Furthermore, if the operating system supports semaphores directly then under certain error conditions they may be more robust than any logical equivalents constructed from mutexes and events — however, this topic is not covered here.

The PIPELINE class is completely 'thread-safe' since it allows multiple writers to call Put() and multiple readers to call Get() without any fear of corruption of the internal data structures within a PIPELINE object — this contrasts with the TRANSFER class introduced in section 4.4 and covered more fully in section 6.2 which can handle only one writer thread and one reader thread. The PIPELINE class consequently supports four different modes of operation:

— one-to-one
— one-to-many
— many-to-one
— many-to-many

For example, in the one-to-many mode a PIPELINE object could be used to allow a single master thread to schedule activities for a team of slave threads — the master thread injects job instructions into the pipeline and these are taken one at a time by the various slave threads as soon as they complete their previous assignment.

5.6 The ARBITRATOR Class

The ARBITRATOR class supports yet another method of transferring data between different threads — it also illustrates a third application of semaphores. The ARBITRATOR class is primarily designed to coordinate the activities of a collection of threads writing to and reading from a shared memory region but it could just as well be used to protect the integrity of any resource whose state can be updated by some threads and queried by others — the basic requirement is that the resource can be modified by only one thread at a time but it can be examined simultaneously by multiple threads. As its name implies the ARBITRATOR class provides an arbitration service for regulating the demands of a resource's writer and reader threads — a separate ARBITRATOR object must be created for each resource requiring arbitration:

```
ARBITRATOR arbitrator;
```

The ARBITRATOR class defines the set of four functions ReaderLock(), ReaderUnlock(), WriterLock() and WriterUnlock() which the writer and reader threads should invoke at the appropriate times. Before it reads data from its resource, a reader thread calls ReaderLock() to prevent a writer thread from

changing the data and after the read operation is complete a corresponding call to
`ReaderUnlock()` is necessary:

```
arbitrator.ReaderLock();
   ...
// reader active
   ...
arbitrator.ReaderUnlock();
```

Note that calling `ReaderLock()` holds up only writer threads — other reader
threads will still be able to invoke `ReaderLock()` successfully for themselves. A
writer thread must similarly call `WriterLock()` before its write operation and
`WriterUnlock()` afterwards:

```
arbitrator.WriterLock();
   ...
// writer active
   ...
arbitrator.WriterUnlock();
```

However, once one thread has completed its call to `WriterLock()` no other locks
by readers or writers will succeed until the matching call to `WriterUnlock()` is
made. The full specification for the ARBITRATOR class is as follows:

```
class ARBITRATOR {
public:
  ARBITRATOR(int);
  ~ARBITRATOR(void);
  void ReaderLock(void);
  void ReaderUnlock(void);
  void WriterLock(void);
  void WriterUnlock(void);
private:
  MUTEX Mutex;
  SEMAPHORE Semaphore;
  int MaxReaders;
};
```

The embedded `Semaphore` object is used to count the number of readers currently
active — since a writer thread must wait for all readers to cease reading before it
starts writing, each reader thread signals the `Semaphore` object just after it stops
reading and so the semaphore counter actually represents the current number of
'inactive' readers. The ARBITRATOR class constructor consequently requires a

`max_readers` parameter to allow it to signal that all the readers are initially inactive:

```
ARBITRATOR::ARBITRATOR(int max_readers) {
  MaxReaders = max_readers;
  for (int i=0; (i<MaxReaders); i++)
    Semaphore.Signal();
}

ARBITRATOR::~ARBITRATOR(void) {}
```

A side-effect of this design is that the number of simultaneously active readers is limited to `max_readers` — if the maximum permissible number of readers are already active and another thread invokes `ReaderLock()` then it will block in the internal call to the `Semaphore` object's `Wait()` function until one of the active threads stops reading:

```
void ARBITRATOR::ReaderLock(void) {
  Mutex.Acquire();
  Mutex.Release();
  Semaphore.Wait();
}
```

The `ReaderLock()` function also temporarily acquires the `Mutex` object to check whether another thread is currently waiting to write — this use of the `Mutex` object is described in more detail below. The `ReaderUnlock()` function simply signals that the thread has finished reading:

```
void ARBITRATOR::ReaderUnlock(void) {
  Semaphore.Signal();
}
```

The `WriterLock()` function is a little more interesting since it must wait for any active readers to stop reading — it must also prevent more than one writer from being active concurrently. As previously explained, the `WriterLock()` function determines when all the readers are inactive by repeatedly calling the `Semaphore` object's `Wait()` function:

```
void ARBITRATOR::WriterLock(void) {
  Mutex.Acquire();
  for (int i=0; (i<MaxReaders); i++)
    Semaphore.Wait();
}
```

The `WriterLock()` function ensures mutual exclusion amongst writer threads by acquiring the `Mutex` object — the corresponding `Release()` call appears in the `WriterUnlock()` function. However, the `Mutex` object also serves another purpose — this fact was mentioned above in connection with the `ReaderLock()` function. Without the `Mutex` object the writer thread could be blocked out by a rapid stream of readers, perhaps waiting indefinitely depending on the fairness of the scheduling algorithm — when one reader signals that it has finished, another reader thread could make a successful call to the `Semaphore` object's `Wait()` function before the writer thread manages to decrement the semaphore count. However with the `Mutex` object present, once the writer thread has acquired the mutex all subsequent calls to `ReaderLock()` will fail in their attempt to temporarily acquire the mutex and so the writer thread will be free to continue as soon as all the current readers make their `ReaderUnlock()` calls. Note that the `Wait()` call in `ReaderLock()` must not precede the `Acquire()` call since this may result in 'deadlock' — a reader could complete the `Wait()` call but then block in `Acquire()` because the writer holds the mutex, but the writer would be blocked too whilst it waits endlessly to decrement the semaphore count to zero. The general topic of deadlock is discussed much more fully in chapter 8.

The `WriterUnlock()` function is fairly straightforward — it opens the way for the reader threads by making multiple calls to the `Semaphore` object `Signal()` function and then releasing its hold on the `Mutex` object:

```
void ARBITRATOR::WriterUnlock(void) {
  for (int i=0; (i<MaxReaders); i++)
    Semaphore.Signal();
  Mutex.Release();
}
```

Although it is most natural to use a mutex to serialize the write operations, here it would be possible to substitute either an event or a semaphore. Initially the writer is inactive so an event would have to start out in the signalled state, then `WriterLock()` would call `Wait()` to move the event to the non-signalled state and `WriterUnlock()` would restore the signalled state — the `ReaderLock()` function calls `Wait()` and `Signal()` for the event to avoid blocking out an aspiring writer. The semaphore alternative would simply imitate the non-signalled and signalled states of the event using 0 and 1 semaphore counter values.

Finally, note that the active writer thread is at liberty to read data from its associated resource and need not call `ReaderLock()` — indeed for some operating systems calling `ReaderLock()` after `WriterLock()` will cause the thread to lock up when it tries to reacquire the `Mutex` object.

5.7 UNIX Implementation

Because the `SYNCH` class paradigm for waiting and signalling closely mimics that defined for UNIX condition variables, it is reasonably easy to implement the `SYNCH` class under UNIX — each `SYNCH` object simply embeds a `pthread_cond_t` condition variable structure as well as an associated `pthread_mutex_t` structure to provide the necessary mutex protection. Since the `SYNCH` class is so versatile this close correlation suggests that the POSIX standard for thread synchronization is indeed well designed.

The complete SYNCH class specification is as follows:

```
synch.h:

#ifndef _SYNCH_HEADER
#define _SYNCH_HEADER

#include "unix.h"
#include <pthread.h>

const int SYNCH_FAIL = 0;
const int SYNCH_OKAY = 1;
const int SYNCH_WAIT = 2;

class SYNCH {
public:
  SYNCH(void);
  virtual ~SYNCH(void);
  int Wait(void* = NULL);
  void Signal(void* = NULL);
  void Broadcast(void* = NULL);
protected:
  virtual int Status(void*);
  virtual int Update(void*);
private:
  pthread_cond_t Event;
  pthread_mutex_t Mutex;
};

#endif
```

As in the UNIX implementation of the EVENT class presented in section 4.6, the SYNCH class constructor initializes the condition variable and mutex whilst the SYNCH class destructor releases these resources for re-use by the operating system:

```
synch.cxx:

#include "unix.h"
#include "synch.h"

SYNCH::SYNCH(void) {
  pthread_cond_init(&Event,(pthread_condattr_t*)NULL);
  pthread_mutex_init(&Mutex,(pthread_mutexattr_t*)NULL);
}

SYNCH::~SYNCH(void) {
  pthread_cond_destroy(&Event);
  pthread_mutex_destroy(&Mutex);
}
```

The SYNCH class Wait() function follows the basic pattern described in section 5.1 but waits on a condition variable rather than an event:

```
int SYNCH::Wait(void* context) {
  pthread_mutex_lock(&Mutex);
  int status = Status(context);
  while (status == SYNCH_WAIT) {
    pthread_cond_wait(&Event,&Mutex);
    status = Status(context);
  }
  pthread_mutex_unlock(&Mutex);
  return (status == SYNCH_OKAY);
}
```

The SYNCH class Wait() function initially calls pthread_mutex_lock() so that Status() can evaluate the current synchronization state under mutex protection — the mutex is finally released by pthread_mutex_unlock(). If Status() indicates that the thread must wait then pthread_cond_wait() is called to wait for a signal to re-evaluate the state — eventually Status() will return SYNCH_OKAY or SYNCH_FAIL and the while loop will be exited. As described in section 4.6 the pthread_cond_wait() function internally releases the mutex just before waiting and then reacquires the mutex after it receives a signal — in particular, the function ensures that the calling thread cannot miss a signal between releasing the mutex and starting to wait. The SYNCH class Signal() function also adheres to the basic pattern discussed in section 5.1 — as with the SYNCH class Wait() function a condition variable replaces the event primitive used in the earlier section:

```
void SYNCH::Signal(void* context) {
  pthread_mutex_lock(&Mutex);
  if (Update(context))
    pthread_cond_signal(&Event);
  pthread_mutex_unlock(&Mutex);
}
```

The SYNCH class Signal() function should be chosen if any single waiting thread will be able to complete its Wait() call — in this situation the pthread_cond_signal() function is ideal since it guarantees to release only one waiting thread and will in general release no more. On the other hand, if several threads may be able to end their wait or if some threads may be unable to do so, then the SYNCH class Broadcast() function is required:

```
void SYNCH::Broadcast(void* context) {
  pthread_mutex_lock(&Mutex);
  if (Update(context))
    pthread_cond_broadcast(&Event);
  pthread_mutex_unlock(&Mutex);
}
```

The `Broadcast()` function differs from the `Signal()` function in that it calls `pthread_cond_broadcast()` instead of `pthread_cond_signal()` and this new function releases all waiting threads to re-evaluate their status although not necessarily, of course, to return from `Wait()`. Finally, the `SYNCH` class provides dummy definitions for its `Status()` and `Update()` virtual functions for use in certain rare circumstances such as prototyping:

```
int SYNCH::Status(void*) {
    return SYNCH_FAIL;
}

int SYNCH::Update(void*) {
    return FALSE;
}
```

However, these functions should definitely be overridden in any derived classes.

5.8 Windows Implementation

Whereas the POSIX standard for UNIX defines only mutexes and condition variables to assist in thread synchronization, Windows provides mutexes, events and semaphores built into the operating system — this section starts with an implementation of the `SEMAPHORE` class constructed using Windows semaphores directly rather than through derivation from the `SYNCH` base class. The specification for this version of the `SEMAPHORE` class is as follows:

```
semaphore.h:

#ifndef _SEMAPHORE_HEADER
#define _SEMAPHORE_HEADER

#include <windows.h>

const int SEMAPHORE_MAX_COUNT = 1000000;

class SEMAPHORE {
public:
    SEMAPHORE(int = 0);
    ~SEMAPHORE(void);
    void Signal(void);
    void Wait(void);
    int Test(void);
private:
    HANDLE Semaphore;
};

#endif
```

The specification is similar to that given in section 5.3 but, as explained there, it ignores the context parameters for the `Signal()` and `Wait()` functions as well as the return parameter from the `Wait()` function. The SEMAPHORE class constructor creates a new Windows semaphore by calling the function `CreateSemaphore()` and then stores the returned handle to this semaphore in the `Semaphore` field:

`semaphore.cxx`:

```
#include <windows.h>
#include "semaphore.h"

SEMAPHORE::SEMAPHORE(int count) {
  Semaphore =
   CreateSemaphore(NULL,SEMAPHORE_MAX_COUNT,count,NULL);
}
```

The third parameter to `CreateSemaphore()` initializes the semaphore count — for a Windows semaphore the count must always remain between zero and some maximum value which is set here to the arbitrarily large constant SEMAPHORE_MAX_COUNT. As discussed in section 3.11 the first and last parameters passed to `CreateSemaphore()` are NULL values. The SEMAPHORE class destructor releases the Windows semaphore by calling `CloseHandle()` on the stored semaphore handle:

```
  SEMAPHORE::~SEMAPHORE(void) {
    CloseHandle(Semaphore);
  }
```

The SEMAPHORE class `Signal()` function increments the semaphore count by 1 with a call to the Windows `ReleaseSemaphore()` function:

```
  void SEMAPHORE::Signal(void) {
    ReleaseSemaphore(Semaphore,1,NULL);
  }
```

The final parameter to `ReleaseSemaphore()` is NULL in this instance but it can be used to retrieve the count held by the Windows semaphore. As for the MUTEX class `Acquire()` and `Acquired()` functions and the EVENT class `Wait()` and `Test()` functions, the generic Windows wait function `WaitForSingleObject()` is used to implement the SEMAPHORE class `Wait()` and `Test()` functions — the blocking `Wait()` function specifies an infinite timeout:

```
  void SEMAPHORE::Wait(void) {
    WaitForSingleObject(Semaphore,INFINITE);
  }
```

And the non-blocking `Test()` function specifies a zero timeout:

```
int SEMAPHORE::Test(void) {
  return WaitForSingleObject(Semaphore,0)!=WAIT_TIMEOUT;
}
```

The SEMAPHORE class is thus easy to implement directly under Windows but the same cannot be said of the SYNCH class — the complication arises in the implementation of the SYNCH class `Broadcast()` function. The condition variable paradigm for signalling which the SYNCH class adopts is essentially equivalent to pulsing an event — first the event is set to its signalled state, then the waiting threads are released and finally the event is returned to the non-signalled state. For the SYNCH class `Signal()` function only one waiting thread needs to be released but for the `Broadcast()` function all waiting threads must be released — these alternatives correspond to the functionality provided by the Windows `PulseEvent()` function for automatic and manual events respectively so perhaps the `Signal()` and `Broadcast()` functions could be implemented using automatic and manual events respectively:

```
void SYNCH::Signal(void* context) {
  WaitForSingleObject(Mutex,INFINITE);
  if (Update(context))
    PulseEvent(Event); // automatic event
  ReleaseMutex(Mutex);
}

void SYNCH::Broadcast(void* context) {
  WaitForSingleObject(Mutex,INFINITE);
  if (Update(context))
    PulseEvent(OtherEvent); // manual event
  ReleaseMutex(Mutex);
}
```

The SYNCH class `Wait()` function would then have to wait for either event to occur by calling the Windows `WaitForMultipleObjects()` function:

```
int SYNCH::Wait(void* context) {
  int status;
  HANDLE events[2] = {Event,OtherEvent};
  do {
    WaitForSingleObject(Mutex,INFINITE);
    status = Status(context);
    ReleaseMutex(Mutex);
    if (status == SYNCH_WAIT)
      WaitForMultipleObjects(2,events,FALSE,INFINITE);
  } while (status == SYNCH_WAIT);
  return (status == SYNCH_OKAY);
}
```

However, there is a bug inherent in this solution. Windows does not provide an equivalent to the POSIX function `pthread_cond_wait()` that atomically releases a mutex and waits on a condition variable — consequently, the SYNCH class `Wait()` function must release its mutex before starting to wait on an event. The bug therefore occurs if the `PulseEvent()` function is called between the mutex being released and the waiting thread starting to wait — in this case the waiter will not be released immediately but instead will be left to wait indefinitely. Of course, the Windows remedy for this bug is to signal the event rather than to pulse it and then to let the built-in memory capability of the event carry the signal across the gap between the mutex release and the start of the wait:

```
int SYNCH::Wait(void* context) {
  int status;
  HANDLE objects[2] = {Mutex,Event};
  do {
    WaitForSingleObject(Mutex,INFINITE);
    status = Status(context);
    if (status == SYNCH_WAIT)
      Waiters++;
    ReleaseMutex(Mutex);
    if (status == SYNCH_WAIT) {
      WaitForMultipleObjects(2,objects,TRUE,INFINITE);
      if (--Runners)
        SetEvent(Event);
      ReleaseMutex(Mutex);
    }
  } while (status == SYNCH_WAIT);
  return (status == SYNCH_OKAY);
}
```

If a thread is about to wait on the event it first increments the `Waiters` field so that the SYNCH class `Broadcast()` function knows how many threads to release — when `Broadcast()` is invoked it turns all the waiters into 'runners' by setting `Waiters` to zero and incrementing the `Runners` field appropriately:

```
void SYNCH::Broadcast(void* context) {
  WaitForSingleObject(Mutex,INFINITE);
  if (Update(context) && Waiters) {
    Runners += Waiters;
    Waiters = 0;
    SetEvent(Event);
  }
  ReleaseMutex(Mutex);
}
```

The Broadcast() function also sets the event which signals to the waiting threads in Wait() — this event must be automatic so that as the waiters are awoken one by one the event is immediately reset and the newly active thread is able to examine the Runners field to determine whether it is the last runner or whether the event should be set again for another runner. The Wait() function must use the Windows function WaitForMultipleObjects() to atomically acquire the Mutex object whenever the Event object is signalled and so avoid interference from the Broadcast() function until a runner has finished processing its signal — a neater alternative would be to replace the event, the mutex and the Runners field with a Windows semaphore but the current approach provides a good introduction to the final design which for the sake of portability is based solely on mutexes and events. The problem of missing a signal has now been solved but there is still another bug. It is intended that the Runners variable will be decremented by the threads currently waiting in the Wait() function — the specification for the Broadcast() function says that it should release exactly all those threads which are waiting when Broadcast() is invoked. However, it is possible that some thread (either one of those released by Broadcast() or a new thread calling the Wait() function) may receive the return value SYNCH_WAIT from Status() and then proceed to consume the Runners count inappropriately — this will prevent one of the other threads that was waiting from being released. Fortunately, this bug is easy to fix — an OtherEvent object is introduced to allow the last runner to be released to signal that the broadcaster can continue:

```
int SYNCH::Wait(void* context) {
  int status;
  do {
    WaitForSingleObject(Mutex,INFINITE);
    status = Status(context);
    if (status == SYNCH_WAIT)
      Waiters++;
    ReleaseMutex(Mutex);
    if (status == SYNCH_WAIT) {
      WaitForSingleObject(Event,INFINITE);
      if (--Runners)
        SetEvent(Event);
      else
        SetEvent(OtherEvent);
    }
  } while (status == SYNCH_WAIT);
  return (status == SYNCH_OKAY);
}
```

In the meantime the broadcasting thread simply keeps hold of the `Mutex` object:

```
void SYNCH::Broadcast(void* context) {
  WaitForSingleObject(Mutex,INFINITE);
  if (Update(context) && Waiters) {
    Runners = Waiters;
    Waiters = 0;
    SetEvent(Event);
    WaitForSingleObject(OtherEvent,INFINITE);
  }
  ReleaseMutex(Mutex);
}
```

Note that `Wait()` no longer needs to protect the `Runners` field with the `Mutex` object since the `Event` object is automatic and so ensures there is only a single runner active at a time — furthermore, no more broadcasts are possible whilst there are runners and so only the runners are currently modifying the `Runners` field. The remainder of the SYNCH class is now relatively straightforward to implement:

```
synch.h:

#ifndef _SYNCH_HEADER
#define _SYNCH_HEADER

#include <windows.h>

const int SYNCH_FAIL = 0;
const int SYNCH_OKAY = 1;
const int SYNCH_WAIT = 2;

class SYNCH {
public:
  SYNCH(void);
  virtual ~SYNCH(void);
  int Wait(void* = NULL);
  void Signal(void* = NULL);
  void Broadcast(void* = NULL);
protected:
  virtual int Status(void*);
  virtual int Update(void*);
private:
  int Waiters;
  int Runners;
  HANDLE Mutex;
  HANDLE Event;
  HANDLE OtherEvent;
};

#endif
```

The SYNCH class constructor creates the necessary Windows mutex and events as well as zeroing the Waiters and Runners fields:

```
synch.cxx:

#include <windows.h>
#include "synch.h"

SYNCH::SYNCH(void) {
  Mutex = CreateMutex(NULL,FALSE,NULL);
  Event = CreateEvent(NULL,FALSE,FALSE,NULL);
  OtherEvent = CreateEvent(NULL,FALSE,FALSE,NULL);
  Waiters = 0;
  Runners = 0;
}
```

The SYNCH class destructor correspondingly destroys all the Windows synchronization objects:

```
SYNCH::~SYNCH(void) {
  CloseHandle(Mutex);
  CloseHandle(Event);
  CloseHandle(OtherEvent);
}
```

The SYNCH class Signal() function is similar to the Broadcast() function but it generates only a single runner each time it is invoked:

```
void SYNCH::Signal(void* context) {
  WaitForSingleObject(Mutex,INFINITE);
  if (Update(context) && Waiters) {
    Runners++;
    Waiters--;
    SetEvent(Event);
    WaitForSingleObject(OtherEvent,INFINITE);
  }
  ReleaseMutex(Mutex);
}
```

Finally, as in the UNIX implementation of the SYNCH class, the Windows implementation provides dummy definitions for the Status() and Update() functions so that 'do-nothing' SYNCH objects can be created if for some reason this is desired:

```
int SYNCH::Status(void*) {
  return SYNCH_FAIL;
}

int SYNCH::Update(void*) {
  return FALSE;
}
```

5.9 Summary

A semaphore is a useful generalization of an event that provides Wait() and Signal() functions to support inter-thread communication — the semaphore contains a counter which is mutex protected to avoid corruption whenever multiple threads attempt to modify its value simultaneously. The semaphore count can assume one of the values 0, 1, 2, ... and may be incremented by calling Signal() or decremented by calling Wait() — if the semaphore count is zero whenever Wait() is invoked then the thread enters its 'Sleeping' state and demands no processor time until Signal() is called. The SEMAPHORE class embodies the functionality of a semaphore and is derived from the SYNCH base class — in addition to the Signal() and Wait() functions, the SEMAPHORE class also supplies the non-blocking function Test() which acts like Wait() but immediately returns FALSE if the semaphore count is zero. The SYNCH class is designed to provide a reliable pattern of thread synchronization that is re-usable in a variety of different situations — the class defines Wait(), Signal() and Broadcast() functions that enable threads to signal to one another and to wait efficiently for these signals. When either Signal() or Broadcast() is invoked the virtual function Update() is called internally to update the state of the synchronization object and to decide whether or not to send a signal — similarly, the SYNCH class Wait() function internally calls the virtual function Status() to examine the state of the object and determine if the calling thread can proceed immediately or if it must wait for a signal. The Update() and Status() functions should be overridden in each derived class to provide the desired synchronization facilities — the derived classes will typically define a set of state variables that are maintained by this pair of functions whilst the Wait(), Signal() and Broadcast() functions also permit context parameters to be passed through to Update() and Status() on a call-by-call basis. The only difference between the SYNCH class Signal() and Broadcast() functions is that the former just guarantees to release a single waiting thread whilst the latter releases all the threads that are waiting — each of the released threads will re-evaluate the current synchronization state by calling Status() but not all these threads will necessarily escape from the Wait() function. If there are no threads waiting in Wait() whenever Signal() or Broadcast() is invoked then neither function sends a signal and the base SYNCH class does not even bother to record the fact that a signal operation was attempted although, of course, each derived class probably will do so in its overriding Update() function. The UNIX implementation of the SYNCH class is relatively straightforward and illustrates the elegance of the design for the POSIX threads standard — on the other hand implementing the SYNCH class under Windows is quite tricky despite the fact that Windows supplies many more facilities for thread synchronization (including semaphores) built into the operating system. A classic application of a semaphore is to monitor the number of essentially identical resources currently available from a pool. The POOL base class provides an example of this usage — derived classes must be implemented to handle particular resource types. The PIPELINE and ARBITRATOR classes, like the BUFFER class of the previous chapter, each support a convenient mechanism for safely transferring data between threads — the PIPELINE class counts the number of items in transit from producers to consumers with a semaphore whilst the ARBITRATOR class uses a semaphore to regulate the activities of multiple reader and writer threads.

6. Objects

Applications written in C++ have traditionally used objects in a 'passive' manner — each C++ object provides a collection of services which may be invoked from external code by calling functions defined in the object's interface. However, in a multi-threaded program C++ objects can be transformed into 'active' entities that perform processing tasks independently of external code — to become active an object simply has to run one or more threads internally. This chapter firstly examines the different patterns of execution flow that are possible with passive and active object paradigms — various implementations of the MUX and DEMUX classes are then described to illustrate the different techniques involved in creating passive or active classes. The key topics covered in the chapter include:

- passive and active C++ classes
- thread execution flow diagrams
- the TRANSFER class
- the MUX and DEMUX classes

The chapter also introduces the TRANSFER_INTERFACE class as another example of utilizing C++ interface classes — this particular interface is designed to allow different objects to communicate via a standardized data exchange mechanism.

6.1 Passive and Active Objects

Despite the fact that they are intended to support multi-threading, virtually all the C++ classes described throughout the book so far illustrate a style of programming that is typical of single-threaded applications — the objects operate in a 'passive' manner providing a collection of services that can be requested by external threads. The basic interaction between an external thread and a passive object is for the thread to call one of the functions supplied by the passive object so that the thread's flow of execution enters the object for the duration of the function — the only difference between a single-threaded program and a multi-threaded one is that in the former case the external thread is always the primary thread whilst in the latter case it may be a secondary thread started by a THREAD object.

The following figure depicts this basic interaction:

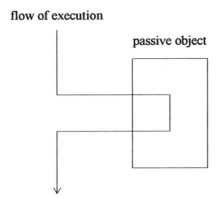

A common variation is for a function called in one passive object (A) to make use of the services provided by other passive objects (B and C):

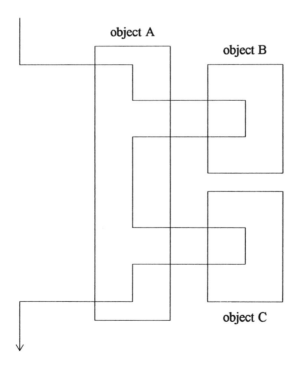

The same pattern also occurs when a number of objects (B and C) register 'callback' functions with some object (A) and this object provides a function to activate the callbacks — when the activation function is invoked the flow of execution passes to each of the registered objects in turn as their callback functions are executed. Another alternative is for a pair of objects to set up a dialogue that transfers the flow of execution back and forth between them:

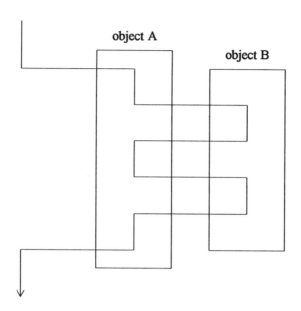

A program with a single thread can support only the passive object paradigm but with multiple threads it becomes possible to create 'active' objects — an active object does not just sit passively waiting for external threads to make use of its services but instead runs internal threads of its own:

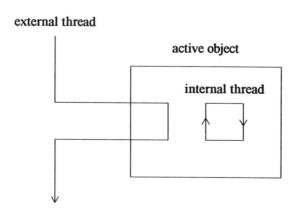

Typically an active object sets its internal threads running in the constructor — for example, the LOOPY object starts its lone internal thread as follows:

```
LOOPY::LOOPY(void) {
   ...
   Start(param);
}
```

Whilst an active object is alive, its internal threads may periodically update the state of the object independently of external influences or alternatively they may wait for instructions from external threads to perform certain processing — in any case, as just depicted, the internal threads often perform their processing in some kind of loop:

```
void* LOOPY::Run(void* param) {
   while (!Quit.Test()) {
      ...
   }
   return NULL;
}
```

Here the loop is terminated when the Quit event is set to its signalled state — the active object destructor is typically responsible for stopping the internal threads:

```
LOOPY::~LOOPY(void) {
   Quit.Signal();
   Wait();
}
```

Finally, note that it is even possible for the internal threads of an active object (A) to adopt the passive object paradigm and make external calls to other objects (B):

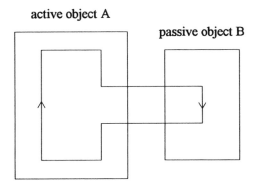

active object A

passive object B

The remaining sections of this chapter develop the MUX and DEMUX classes to further illustrate the differences between passive and active objects.

6.2 The TRANSFER Class

The TRANSFER class was first introduced in section 4.4 as a straightforward wrapper for the BUFFER class — this section upgrades the definition of the TRANSFER class to provide a fully functional implementation. To permit the underlying transfer mechanism to be easily changed, the TRANSFER class is actually derived from the TRANSFER_INTERFACE base class — so, for example, the CHANNEL class described in section 10.2 could be substituted for the BUFFER class in order to create a derived transfer class capable of providing network communications instead of in-process buffering. As its name suggests the TRANSFER_INTERFACE class is an 'interface class' (see section 3.6) and so defines a functional interface by including only pure virtual functions in its specification and providing no implementation details:

```
class TRANSFER_INTERFACE {
public:
  virtual int Send(char*,int) = 0;
  virtual int Receive(char**,int*) = 0;
  virtual void Break(void) = 0;
};
```

The Send() function receives a pointer to a block of data to be sent plus the length of the data — the Receive() function takes pointers to similar parameters for the received data block and fills in the appropriate values before returning. The data block passed to Send() must be created by the caller but will be destroyed by the callee — correspondingly, the Receive() function returns a pointer to a newly allocated block of memory which must be freed by the caller after the data has been processed. The Send() and Receive() functions may both block indefinitely and so the Break() function is supplied to allow calls to these functions to be interrupted whenever necessary — the Send() and Receive() functions generally return a TRUE status value but they return FALSE to indicate that they have been interrupted. The transfer interface defined by the TRANSFER_INTERFACE class allows data to be passed from object to object in a standardized manner — the underlying mechanisms used by the objects to actually transfer the data become relatively unimportant. One possible arrangement is illustrated by the following figure:

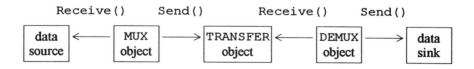

Here the TRANSFER class services calls to both its Send() and Receive() functions whilst the MUX object queries data sources by calling their Receive() function and the DEMUX object delivers data by calling the Send() function of

data sinks. In general, one object in a communications chain can call Receive()
to obtain data from its predecessor and then call Send() to pass the data along to
its successor — alternatively an object could be interrogated for data by having its
own Receive() function called or be handed data through its Send() function.

The full specification for the TRANSFER class is as follows:

```
class TRANSFER : public TRANSFER_INTERFACE {
public:
  TRANSFER(void);
  virtual ~TRANSFER(void);
  virtual int Send(char*,int);
  virtual int Receive(char**,int*);
  virtual void Break(void);
private:
  BUFFER Buffer;
  MUTEX Mutex;
  EVENT Quit;
};
```

The constructor simply ensures that Quit is a manual EVENT object whilst the
destructor performs no action — external code must ensure that there are no
Send() or Receive() calls still in progress when the TRANSFER object is
destroyed.

```
TRANSFER::TRANSFER(void) : Quit(FALSE) {}

TRANSFER::~TRANSFER(void) {}
```

The Send() and Receive() functions inherit their functional specification from
the TRANSFER_INTERFACE base class but must be implemented by the
TRANSFER class. As noted in section 4.4 the TRANSFER class relies on a simple
communication protocol that prefixes each message with its length:

```
int TRANSFER::Send(char* data,int length) {
  int status = FALSE;
  Mutex.Acquire();
  if (!Quit.Test() && (length>0)) {
    Buffer.WriteData((char*)&length,sizeof(int));
    Buffer.WriteData(data,length);
    status = TRUE;
  }
  Mutex.Release();
  delete [] data;
  return status;
}
```

Unlike the implementation described in section 4.4, the TRANSFER class Send()
function now checks the Quit event before actually sending the data — the
function also avoids sending a message of zero length since this is used to mark the
termination of the transfer. The Break() function sets the state of the Quit event
to 'signalled' and sends a zero length message to the receiver — this latter action
ensures that the receiver will not block forever waiting for data once the sender has
ceased transmitting.

```
void TRANSFER::Break(void) {
  int length = 0;
  Mutex.Acquire();
  if (!Quit.Test()) {
    Quit.Signal();
    Buffer.WriteData((char*)&length,sizeof(int));
  }
  Mutex.Release();
}
```

The Mutex object serves the TRANSFER class in two ways. Firstly, it ensures
atomicity of the state transition which occurs when Break() is invoked — in
particular, the zero length termination message will definitely be the last one
transmitted. Secondly, the Mutex object serializes use of the communications
channel by the TRANSFER class Send() function — recall that the BUFFER class
of section 4.4 is designed to work with only a single writer and so messages from
different data sources must be sent one after the other. At the receiver side, the
length prefix determines the size of the memory block that must be allocated to
hold the received data:

```
int TRANSFER::Receive(char** data,int* length) {
  int status = FALSE;
  if (!Quit.Test()) {
    Buffer.ReadData((char*)length,sizeof(int));
    if (*length > 0) {
      *data = new char[*length];
      Buffer.ReadData(*data,*length);
      status = TRUE;
    }
  }
  return status;
}
```

The TRANSFER class implementation of the Break() function is not perfect — it
assumes that the receiver will continuously pull data from the buffer so that
eventually any pending Send() call will succeed and the Break() function will

get a chance to set the Quit event flag and send its termination message to the receiver. Ideally the BUFFER class would support some method of breaking blocked threads out of its WriteData() and ReadData() functions and so enable the TRANSFER class Break() function to abort an outstanding send or receive operation immediately — the CHANNEL class described in section 10.2 provides an example of this technique where the sending and receiving threads block not on events but in calls to operating system functions for network communications.

6.3 Passive MUX Sender

The MUX and DEMUX classes respectively perform multiplexing and demultiplexing operations that allow communication between multiple data sources and data sinks through a single channel — the previous section illustrated this arrangement with a TRANSFER object acting as the communications channel. In a real application the MUX and DEMUX objects would probably be combined but they are kept separate here to avoid complicating the discussion — this section and the next respectively detail passive MUX objects and active DEMUX objects whilst section 6.5 describes an implementation of the MUX class that utilizes active MUX objects. The passive MUX class has the following specification:

```
class MUX {
public:
  MUX(TRANSFER_INTERFACE*);
  ~MUX(void);
  void Send(TRANSFER_INTERFACE*,int);
private:
  TRANSFER_INTERFACE* Transfer;
};
```

The constructor stores a pointer to a transfer object whilst the destructor does nothing:

```
MUX::MUX(TRANSFER_INTERFACE* transfer) {
  Transfer = transfer;
}

MUX::~MUX(void) {}
```

Because the MUX object only refers to its TRANSFER object through a TRANSFER_INTERFACE* pointer, it is easy to update the underlying transfer mechanism simply by substituting another type of transfer object — as previously noted the CHANNEL class could be wrapped in another class derived from TRANSFER_INTERFACE to provide an example where the transfer occurs via a network connection.

A data source calls the MUX class Send() function whenever it wants to transfer data to a data sink:

```
void MUX::Send(TRANSFER_INTERFACE* source,int sink) {
  char* message;
  char* data;
  int length;
  source->Receive(&data,&length);
  message = new char[length+sizeof(int)];
  *(int*)message = sink;
  memcpy(message+sizeof(int),data,length);
  length += sizeof(int);
  Transfer->Send(message,length);
  delete [] data;
}
```

The data source passes its own TRANSFER_INTERFACE* pointer to the Send() function to request a 'callback' — the Send() function retrieves the data from the source object by calling the source's Receive() function using the TRANSFER_INTERFACE* pointer. The MUX class Send() function thus serves as an example of the single-threaded interaction depicted in section 6.1 where two passive objects engage in a dialogue — in this case it is the data source and the MUX object that are conversing, with the data source invoking the MUX object's Send() function and the MUX object making a nested call to the data source's Receive() function:

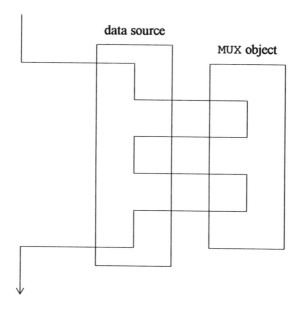

In the call to the MUX class Send() function the destination sink object is specified using a pre-arranged integer identifier since, in general, the data source cannot obtain a TRANSFER_INTERFACE* pointer for the data sink. The Send() function packages up the data as a message placing the sink identifier in the message header:

	header	body
message	id	data

In particular, this allows the sink identifier in the header and the data in the body of the message to be sent using a single call to the TRANSFER class Send() function — this point is important because the Transfer object does not guarantee that multiple Send() calls will be executed as an atomic unit. An alternative approach would be to send the sink identifier and data using separate Send() calls and to ensure atomicity with a MUTEX object embedded in the MUX object.

6.4 Active DEMUX Receiver

The DEMUX object sits at the other end of the communications channel from the MUX object — whereas the MUX object receives messages from the data sources and puts them into the channel, the DEMUX object pulls the messages from the channel and distributes them to the data sinks. However, a more important difference in the context of this chapter is that the MUX object is passive but the DEMUX object is active — the data sources provide the external threads to send messages but the DEMUX object runs an internal thread to receive the messages. The full specification for the DEMUX class is as follows:

```
const int DEMUX_MAX_SINKS = 100;

class DEMUX : public THREAD {
public:
  DEMUX(TRANSFER_INTERFACE*);
  virtual ~DEMUX(void);
  void Register(TRANSFER_INTERFACE*,int);
  void Unregister(int);
protected:
  virtual void* Run(void*);
private:
  TRANSFER_INTERFACE* Transfer;
  TRANSFER_INTERFACE* Sinks[DEMUX_MAX_SINKS];
  int Identifiers[DEMUX_MAX_SINKS];
  int SinkCount;
  MUTEX Mutex;
};
```

Each DEMUX object also supplies Register() and Unregister() functions so that the data sinks can inform it when they wish to receive messages and which identifier value they will be using — the DEMUX object matches the sink identifiers from incoming messages with all those currently registered in order to determine where to deliver the data. The DEMUX object embeds a MUTEX object to protect the data structures used by the registration functions — multiple threads can simultaneously call the Register() and Unregister() functions without fear of corruption. As with the MUX class, the DEMUX class constructor accepts a pointer to a transfer object — the constructor also sets the SinkCount field to zero and starts the DEMUX object's internal thread:

```
DEMUX::DEMUX(TRANSFER_INTERFACE* transfer) {
  Transfer = transfer;
  SinkCount = 0;
  Start();
}
```

Of course, the MUX and DEMUX constructors must be passed a pointer to the same transfer object — the following code is typical:

```
TRANSFER transfer;
MUX mux(&transfer);
DEMUX demux(&transfer);
```

The registration details passed by the data sinks to the DEMUX class Register() function are stored within the DEMUX object in the Sinks and Identifiers arrays — the Sinks array holds TRANSFER_INTERFACE* pointers that reference the various data sinks whilst the Identifiers array contains the corresponding identifiers. The Register() function is implemented as follows:

```
void DEMUX::Register(TRANSFER_INTERFACE* sink, int id)
{
  Mutex.Acquire();
  if (SinkCount < DEMUX_MAX_SINKS) {
    Sinks[SinkCount] = sink;
    Identifiers[SinkCount++] = id;
  }
  Mutex.Release();
}
```

Providing there is room, the latest set of registration details is simply appended to the Sinks and Identifiers arrays — conversely, the Unregister()

function scans the Identifiers array looking for the correct set of registration
details to remove:

```
void DEMUX::Unregister(int id) {
  int i;
  Mutex.Acquire();
  for (i=0; (i<SinkCount); i++)
    if (id == Identifiers[i])
      break;
  if (i < SinkCount)
    SinkCount--;
  for ( ; (i<SinkCount); i++) {
    Sinks[i] = Sinks[i+1];
    Identifiers[i] = Identifiers[i+1];
  }
  Mutex.Release();
}
```

Any details stored after the deleted item are shuffled along to fill up the gap.
Whereas the Register() and Unregister() functions are called by the
external threads from the data sink objects, the internal thread of the DEMUX object
executes the DEMUX class Run() function:

```
void* DEMUX::Run(void*) {
  char* message;
  char* data;
  int length;
  int id;
  int i;
  while (Transfer->Receive(&message,&length)) {
    id = *(int*)message;
    Mutex.Acquire();
    for (i=0; (i<SinkCount); i++)
      if (id == Identifiers[i])
        break;
    if (i < SinkCount) {
      length -= sizeof(int);
      data = new char[length];
      memcpy(data,message+sizeof(int),length);
      Sinks[i]->Send(data,length);
    }
    Mutex.Release();
    delete [] message;
  }
  return NULL;
}
```

The Run() function loops around receiving messages from the Transfer object until the TRANSFER class Receive() function returns FALSE — this will happen whenever the TRANSFER class Break() function has been called for the Transfer object. Upon receipt of a message the Run() function extracts the sink identifier from the message header and then scans the Identifiers array looking for a data sink which is currently registered with this identifier — the search is mutex protected to coordinate with the Register() and Unregister() calls made by the data sinks. If a match is found then the data is passed along to the appropriate data sink by calling its Send() function — otherwise the message is simply discarded. The DEMUX class destructor calls the Transfer object's Break() function to break the Run() function out of its endless loop and then waits for the DEMUX object's internal thread to terminate:

```
DEMUX::~DEMUX(void) {
  Transfer->Break();
  Wait();
}
```

The DEMUX class provides one good example of an active class — the next section illustrates how the passive MUX class of the previous section can be converted into another example of an active class.

6.5 Active MUX Sender

The operation of the MUX class described here is very similar to that of the passive MUX class from section 6.3 — the main difference is that now when a data source calls Send() it registers a callback that is actually executed by the internal thread which the active MUX object is running. The full specification for the active MUX class is as follows:

```
class MUX : public THREAD {
public:
  MUX(TRANSFER_INTERFACE*);
  ~MUX(void);
  void Send(TRANSFER_INTERFACE*,int);
protected:
  virtual void* Run(void*);
private:
  void Transmit(TRANSFER_INTERFACE*,int);
  TRANSFER_INTERFACE* Transfer;
  PIPELINE Pipeline;
};
```

The interface visible to external code (comprising the constructor, the destructor and the Send() function) is identical to that of the passive MUX class.

Furthermore, the active MUX class constructor has the same implementation as the passive class version except that it also starts an internal thread:

```
MUX::MUX(TRANSFER_INTERFACE* transfer) {
  Transfer = transfer;
  Start();
}
```

The implementation of the active MUX class Send() function, however, is quite different from the passive class version:

```
void MUX::Send(TRANSFER_INTERFACE* source,int sink) {
  MUX_INFO* info = new MUX_INFO;
  info->Source = source;
  info->Sink = sink;
  Pipeline.Put(info);
}
```

Instead of the data being passed directly to the Transfer object, the data source's TRANSFER_INTERFACE* pointer and the data sink identifier are bundled into a MUX_INFO structure which is then added to an internal pipeline — the MUX_INFO structure has the following layout:

```
struct MUX_INFO {
  TRANSFER_INTERFACE* Source;
  int Sink;
};
```

At the far end of the pipeline, the various requests from the data sources are extracted by the active MUX object's internal thread as it executes its Run() function:

```
void* MUX::Run(void*) {
  MUX_INFO* info;
  while (info = (MUX_INFO*)(Pipeline.Get())) {
    Transmit(info->Source,info->Sink);
    delete info;
  }
  return NULL;
}
```

The Run() function loops continuously pulling the send requests from the pipeline and processing them by calling the MUX class Transmit() function.

In fact the active MUX class Transmit() function is identical to the passive MUX class Send() function:

```
void MUX::Transmit(TRANSFER_INTERFACE* source,int sink)
{
    char* message;
    char* data;
    int length;
    source->Receive(&data,&length);
    message = new char[length+sizeof(int)];
    *(int*)message = sink;
    memcpy(message+sizeof(int),data,length);
    length +=sizeof(int);
    Transfer->Send(message,length);
    delete [] data;
}
```

In summary, the data sources now request data transfers by registering callbacks that are subsequently handled by the MUX object's internal thread — the flow of execution combines two of the patterns previously illustrated in section 6.1:

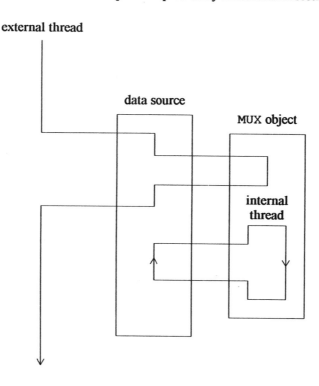

The MUX class Run() function will continue to loop until it discovers a NULL pointer in the pipeline — the MUX class destructor is responsible for placing the NULL pointer there:

```
MUX::~MUX(void) {
  Pipeline.Put(NULL);
  Transfer->Break();
  Wait();
}
```

The destructor also calls the Transfer object's Break() function in case the internal thread is blocked whilst attempting a transfer — once the communications channel has been broken the MUX class Run() function will loop quickly round discarding items from the pipeline until it finds the NULL pointer. Ideally the data sources should cease calling the MUX class Send() function well before the MUX object is destroyed and so there ought to be no pipeline items following the NULL pointer — however, even if the Send() function does manage to sneak the odd item into the pipeline after the destructor inserts its NULL pointer then these items will be deleted by the PIPELINE destructor.

6.6 Summary

A passive object provides a collection of services which may be executed by external threads as they call functions in the object's interface — by contrast, an active object runs one or more internal threads that allow the object to perform processing independently of external code. Whether dealing with passive or active objects, it is possible to identify a variety of fundamental patterns for the flow of thread execution. The basic form of interaction between an external thread and a passive object is for the flow of execution to enter the object for the duration of a function call — conversely, a simple design for an active object is to have an internal thread loop around executing code contained entirely within the object. Variations on these two themes are certainly possible with, for example, the flow of execution for an external thread weaving back and forth between a pair of passive objects or alternatively the internal thread of an active object invoking a callback function previously registered by an external thread from another object. The MUX and DEMUX classes illustrate some of the different techniques for implementing passive and active C++ classes — this pair of classes respectively incorporate multiplexing and demultiplexing facilities to enable communication between multiple data sources and data sinks through a single connecting channel. In particular, the passive MUX object handles the send requests from the various data sources synchronously within the execution flow of the external threads whereas the active MUX object passes the requests through a pipeline to an internal thread for asynchronous transmission — on the receiver side the internal thread of the DEMUX object uses data sink identifiers in the message headers to determine how to distribute the received data. The flow of data from the data sources to the MUX object and across the communications channel to the DEMUX object for eventual delivery to the data sinks is achieved using the standardized data transfer interface defined by the TRANSFER_INTERFACE class. This interface consists of the three functions Send(), Receive() and Break() which serve to hide the actual transfer mechanisms involved at each stage. The Send() function should be passed a pointer to a newly allocated data buffer along with the data length — the callee is responsible for deleting the buffer after it has been processed. Conversely, the Receive() function returns the length of the received data and a pointer to a memory block that holds the data — in this case it is the caller of the Receive() function that must release the memory when it is no longer needed. In general, both of the Send() and Receive() functions may block indefinitely — the TRANSFER_INTERFACE class supplies the Break() function to break threads out of any Send() or Receive() calls currently in progress and to cause subsequent calls to these functions to fail without blocking. The TRANSFER class illustrates one concrete implementation of the transfer interface based on the in-process buffering functionality of the BUFFER class — the CHANNEL class defined in a later chapter could easily be wrapped by another transfer class to permit multiplexed communications across a network connection.

7. Keys

All the threads within a process share the same program code — for two threads to perform different processing they can either execute separate portions of the shared code or alternatively they can run exactly the same code but differentiate their behaviours using other mechanisms. A common technique is for the threads to invoke the same function but to pass in different parameters — for example, the THREAD class Run() function has a parameter that allows otherwise identical threads to particularize their processing. This chapter introduces the notion of using a 'key' as an alternative to parameters for passing thread-specific data from one function to another — a key is essentially a variable that assumes different values when used by different threads and is commonly used to hold pointers to 'thread-specific storage' allocated in dynamic memory. Whenever different threads run shared code that references a key they can perform 'thread-specific processing' which is dependent on the value of the key. Another situation where different threads running the same code must act differently occurs when the shared code performs initialization that should only be executed by the first thread to encounter the code — this chapter covers a number of standard techniques for implementing such 'one-time initialization' requirements. The KEY class and the ONCE class respectively embody keys and one-time initialization in an operating system independent manner. The main topics covered by this chapter include:

— thread-specific storage
— the KEY class
— one-time initialization
— the ONCE class
— implementation details for UNIX and Windows

The chapter also illustrates how to use keys to implement thread identifiers for the THREAD class whenever this functionality is not supported directly by the operating system — a specific implementation for a POSIX compliant system is presented but this can easily be generalized to other environments.

7.1 Thread-Specific Storage

The notion that dynamically allocated memory could be shared by all the threads in a process or alternatively partitioned into thread-specific memory regions was first introduced in section 2.2 — the first possibility, whereby dynamic memory constitutes a process-wide shared resource, is illustrated in the following figure:

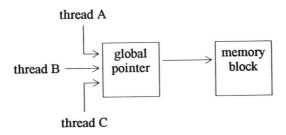

Here threads A, B and C all use the same global pointer to reference the block of dynamic memory. The second possibility is for dynamic memory to be partitioned into different regions each used by a separate thread — in this case the threads A, B and C would replace the shared global pointer variable with thread-specific local pointer variables that reference different blocks of dynamic memory:

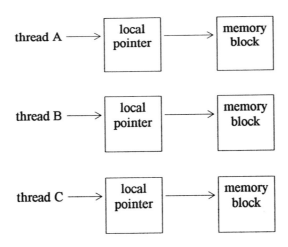

As noted in section 2.2 the former approach provides a shared memory resource that is long-lived whilst the latter permits the storage to be thread-specific but at the expense of using pointers which are only valid for the duration of a function call — to create thread-specific storage with long-lived pointers requires the use of a 'key'. A key is essentially a global pointer variable whose value is thread-specific — when different threads use the pointer variable provided by exactly the same key they actually end up referencing a different block of dynamic memory.

The implementation of a key is illustrated in the following figure:

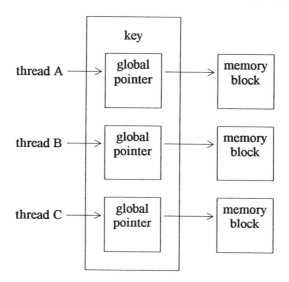

As discussed here keys are generally required to reference thread-specific storage in dynamic memory but they can also be applied to store thread-specific data directly — the data is simply stored as a **void*** pointer through the appropriate use of casting. The next section describes the KEY class which encapsulates the functionality of a key whilst later sections in the chapter contain some additional examples of techniques for working with keys.

7.2 The KEY Class

The KEY class hides the differences in the implementation details of key functionality between operating systems — the interface provided by the KEY class is straightforward:

```
class KEY {
public:
  KEY(void);
  ~KEY(void);
  void Set(void*);
  void* Get(void);
     ...
};
```

As with MUTEX and EVENT classes, the KEY class constructor and destructor respectively initialize and release operating system resources associated with a key. The KEY class Set() and Get() functions allow the key's thread-specific **void*** value to be manipulated by external code — before the first call to Set() is made the Get() function is guaranteed to return a NULL value. As for mutexes

and events, a single thread must create and destroy each key but whilst the key
exists any number of threads can store their thread-specific data using it — the
following code fragment illustrates a typical usage of a key:

thread A   **thread B**
                .   .
```
Key.Set((void*)data_A);        Key.Set((void*)data_B);
```
                .   .
```
ProcessData();                 ProcessData();
```
                .   .

Inside the `ProcessData()` function the `Key` object is used to retrieve the
thread-specific data:

```
void ProcessData(void) {
  void* data = Key.Get();
  // process data
}
```

The code within the `ProcessData()` function is the same for all threads but
since the `Key` object's `Get()` function will return different values for different
threads then the actual processing performed by `ProcessData()` will be
thread-specific — in other words, a key enables 'thread-specific processing' to be
performed. Of course, passing data on the stack as function parameters achieves
much the same effect as using a key:

```
void ProcessData(void* data) {
  // process data
}
```

Conversely, a key provides a method of passing thread-specific data to a function
whenever the parameter mechanism is unavailable — for example, suppose the
SYNCH base class of section 5.2 does not provide context parameters for its various
functions and that the MULTI_EVENT class is to be derived from the base class to
allow multiple events to be signalled or waited upon in combination:

```
class MULTI_EVENT : public SYNCH {
public:
  void Signal(int);
    ...
protected:
  virtual int Update(void*);
    ...
private:
  KEY Key;
  int Active[MULTI_EVENT_MAX_EVENTS];
    ...
};
```

The MULTI_EVENT class Signal() function takes a parameter to indicate which event to signal:

```
void MULTI_EVENT::Signal(int event) {
  Key.Set((void*)event);
  Broadcast();
}
```

The event identifier is stored as thread-specific data within the Key object and then Broadcast() is invoked to wake up all threads that may be waiting for this event to be signalled — the base class Broadcast() function will call the overriding version of Update() defined by the MULTI_EVENT class:

```
int MULTI_EVENT::Update(void*) {
  int event = (int)(long)(Key.Get());
  if (Active[event] == FALSE) {
    Active[event] = TRUE;
    return TRUE;
  }
  return FALSE;
}
```

The Update() function extracts the data from the Key object and sets the appropriate event to its signalled state — this is an example of the thread-specific data being stored directly within the key rather than in dynamic memory referenced by the key. If the event was previously non-signalled then there may be some threads waiting for it to be signalled and so Update() returns TRUE to indicate that the Broadcast() function should indeed awake all waiting threads — if the event is already signalled then no threads can be waiting on it yet and so the broadcast is unnecessary. A full implementation of the MULTI_EVENT class which does use the SYNCH class context parameters is described in chapter 9.

7.3 Thread Identifiers

The UNIX implementation of the THREAD class presented in section 2.5 failed to fully cover the THREAD class GetThreadID() and GetCurrentThreadID() functions — the former function obtains the ID of the thread associated with a particular THREAD object whilst the latter returns the ID of the thread invoking the function. In this section an implementation of thread identifiers based on keys is described — the details are relevant to a POSIX environment but the general approach could easily be applied to other operating systems if required.

The first step is to add the static fields NextThreadID, Mutex and Key
to the THREAD class along with a GetNextThreadID() helper function:

```cpp
static void* ThreadFunction(void*);

class THREAD {
friend void* ThreadFunction(void*);
public:
  THREAD(void);
  virtual ~THREAD(void);
  int Start(void* = NULL);
  void Detach(void);
  void* Wait(void);
  void Stop(void);
  unsigned int GetThreadID(void);
  static unsigned int GetCurrentThreadID(void);
  static void Sleep(int);
protected:
  virtual void* Run(void*);
private:
  unsigned int GetNextThreadID(void);
  static unsigned int NextThreadID;
  static MUTEX Mutex;
  static KEY Key;
  pthread_t ThreadHandle;
  unsigned int ThreadID;
  int Started;
  int Detached;
  void* Param;
};
```

The NextThreadID and Mutex fields are used by the new THREAD class
function GetNextThreadID() to supply a sequence of unique ID values for the
various secondary threads as they are created:

```cpp
unsigned int THREAD::GetNextThreadID(void) {
  Mutex.Acquire();
  unsigned int thread_id = ++NextThreadID;
  Mutex.Release();
  return thread_id;
}
```

The GetNextThreadID() function is called by the THREAD class Start()

function to assign a value to the object's `ThreadID` field just before `pthread_create()` is invoked to create the new thread:

```
int THREAD::Start(void* param) {
  if (!Started) {
    pthread_attr_t attributes;
    pthread_attr_init(&attributes);
    if (Detached)
      pthread_attr_setdetachstate(&attributes,
                          PTHREAD_CREATE_DETACHED);
    Param = param;
    ThreadID = GetNextThreadID();
    if (pthread_create(&ThreadHandle,&attributes,
                    ThreadFunction,this) == 0)
      Started = TRUE;
    pthread_attr_destroy(&attributes);
  }
  return Started;
}
```

Note that the `ThreadID` field must be set before the fork in execution flow so that it will be available to both the thread creating the new thread and the new thread itself — if the `ThreadID` field is set by either thread after the fork then the other thread may attempt to use its value before it is set. The only possible defect with this approach is that if `pthread_create()` fails the allocated thread ID will remain unused — if thread identifiers are assigned by the operating system they will typically only be allocated whenever the thread creation function succeeds. Anyway, the `NextThreadID` counter and the `Mutex` object which protects it must be initialized by the following declaration statements:

```
unsigned int THREAD::NextThreadID = 0;
MUTEX THREAD::Mutex;
```

The initialization is performed at program start-up before the `main()` function is invoked. Since the system just uses the primary thread to execute these declaration statements this is actually an example of a technique for ensuring that initialization code is run exactly once by a single thread — the following section discusses the topic of 'one-time initialization' in much more detail. The THREAD class Key object must also be initialized in a similar manner:

```
KEY THREAD::Key;
```

The `Key` object is used to store a pointer to the THREAD object associated with a

newly created thread — the value of the key for the primary thread defaults to
NULL but for the secondary threads it is set by ThreadFunction() as follows:

```
static void* ThreadFunction(void* object) {
  THREAD* thread = (THREAD*)object;
  thread->Key.Set(object);
  return thread->Run(thread->Param);
}
```

The identifier for a thread associated with a particular THREAD object can be found
by calling the object's GetThreadID() function:

```
unsigned int THREAD::GetThreadID(void) {
  return ThreadID;
}
```

The thread identifier belonging to a thread which invokes the function
GetCurrentThreadID() is determined by retrieving the associated THREAD
object from the key and calling that object's GetThreadID() function —
a NULL value for the key indicates that the primary thread has invoked
GetCurrentThreadID() and so a thread identifier value of zero is returned:

```
unsigned int THREAD::GetCurrentThreadID(void) {
  THREAD* thread = (THREAD*)Key.Get();
  return (thread ? thread->GetThreadID() : 0);
}
```

Thread identifiers, just like keys, provide a mechanism for performing
thread-specific processing — the following example illustrates the basic technique:

```
unsigned int id = THREAD::GetCurrentThreadID();
switch (id) {
case 0:
  printf("Primary Thread");
  break;
default:
  printf("Secondary Thread [%u]",id);
  break;
}
```

In a real application the print statements would, of course, be replaced with code
specific to a particular thread.

7.4 One-Time Initialization

A resource that is shared by multiple threads often needs to be initialized exactly
once by a single thread — such 'one-time initialization' is required, for example,
by objects from the KEY class defined in section 7.2 and also by thread
synchronization primitives such as MUTEX and EVENT objects. As noted in the

previous section one method of performing one-time initialization is to rely on the declaration statements for static fields of a class — a slight variation involves using global variables instead of class fields but this alternative is not particularly object oriented unless, of course, the global variable happens to hold an object. In any case the initialization is performed at start-up before the main() function is invoked — the system guarantees that only the primary thread will execute the declarations although, of course, this activity may entail the creation of secondary threads. Using this approach the resource can be initialized directly (as with the KEY object embedded within the THREAD class from the previous section) or alternatively the start-up code can just set a flag which is subsequently examined under mutex protection to determine whether or not the full initialization has been performed yet — for example, the DEMO class incorporates the static Flag and Mutex fields:

```
class DEMO {
    ...
private:
  void Initialize(void);
  static int Flag;
  static MUTEX Mutex;
};
```

At start-up the Flag field is initialized with the value TRUE and the Mutex object is also created:

```
int DEMO::Flag = TRUE;
MUTEX DEMO::Mutex;
```

Whenever external code requests services of a DEMO object, it ensures that the class has been properly initialized by calling the helper function Initialize() internally:

```
void DEMO::Initialize(void) {
  Mutex.Acquire();
  if (Flag) {
    // initialize DEMO class
    Flag = FALSE;
  }
  Mutex.Release();
}
```

The flag is reset to FALSE within the mutex block to ensure that the class is only initialized once.

Similar techniques involving non-static class fields perform the one-time initialization not at program start-up but when the containing object is created — in this case the initialization occurs either as part of the process of creating the object's fields or alternatively when the object's constructor is executed. The initialization applies to the individual object being created rather than to the class

as a whole — for example, if the constructor only performs partial initialization by
setting a flag then the object's equivalent of the DEMO class Initialize()
function executes one-time initialization code not for the whole class but for the
individual object. Furthermore, whereas with static fields the system automatically
performs the initialization in a single-threaded manner, with non-static fields the
program must provide the thread synchronization necessary to coordinate the object
creation process with the activity of other threads. The 'flag and mutex' mechanism
used by the DEMO class Initialize() function could be applied here but some
operating systems also supply facilities that are specifically designed to assist in
ensuring one-time initialization of resources — the ONCE class described in the
next section embodies this functionality.

7.5 The ONCE Class

When initialization is performed at program start-up the system ensures it is
executed exactly once by the primary thread. However, if initialization is left until
after the main() function has been invoked then it is possible for multiple threads
to attempt to run the initialization code concurrently — if one-time initialization is
required then the program must provide the necessary thread synchronization. The
ONCE class is designed specifically to support one-time initialization after program
start-up and has the following class specification:

```
typedef void ONCE_FUNCTION(void);

class ONCE {
public:
  ONCE(void);
  ~ONCE(void);
  void Execute(ONCE_FUNCTION*);
      ...
};
```

Curiously, each ONCE object itself requires one-time initialization when it is
created — since the ONCE class constructor contains the relevant code this is easily
achieved using any of the techniques previously described. For example, the DEMO
class could be modified to embed a ONCE object as a static field which is then
initialized as follows:

```
ONCE DEMO::Once;
```

The DEMO class Initialize() function subsequently calls the ONCE object's
Execute() function to execute the one-time initialization code for the DEMO
class:

```
void DEMO::Initialize(void) {
  Once.Execute(Init);
}
```

The Init() function is a global function which meets the functional specification defined in the **typedef** statement for ONCE_FUNCTION — Init() must take no parameters and have no return value. The initialization code for the DEMO class is actually contained within the Init() function:

```
void Init(void) {
  // initialize DEMO class
}
```

The ONCE class Execute() function ensures that Init() will be called only once and that it is executed by the first thread to successfully call the Execute() function. Any other threads which call Execute() whilst the first thread is still performing the initialization will block until the first thread completes its work — thereafter, all calls to Execute() have no effect and so Init() is not called again. The ONCE class thus provides a convenient mechanism for performing one-time initialization of a shared resource after program start-up. One possible application might be where the initialization actually depends on which thread happens to execute it — a rudimentary example of such thread-specific processing is illustrated by the following Init() function:

```
void Init(void) {
  printf("Thread %u Initializing ...",
                  THREAD::GetCurrentThreadID());
}
```

Here the initialization routine simply prints out the ID of the thread running Init() but as shown in section 7.3 the code executed by Init() could change completely according to the value of the thread identifier.

7.6 UNIX Implementation

The POSIX standard for UNIX directly supports both keys and one-time initialization — the KEY class simply needs to embed a pthread_key_t structure within each KEY object:

```
class KEY {
public:
  KEY(void);
  ~KEY(void);
  void Set(void*);
  void* Get(void);
private:
  pthread_key_t Key;
};
```

The KEY class constructor creates a key using the `pthread_key_create()` function whilst the destructor deletes the key with the `pthread_key_delete()` function:

```
KEY::KEY(void) {
  pthread_key_create(&Key,(void(*)(void*))NULL);
}

KEY::~KEY(void) {
  pthread_key_delete(Key);
}
```

The value of the key in any thread is always set to NULL at creation — the second parameter to `pthread_key_create()` does not specify the initial value of the key but instead allows an error handling clean-up routine to be installed if desired. The KEY class `Set()` and `Get()` functions likewise just call the operating system functions `pthread_setspecific()` and `pthread_getspecific()` to store and retrieve values for the key associated with a particular KEY object:

```
void KEY::Set(void* value) {
  pthread_setspecific(Key,value);
}

void* KEY::Get(void) {
  return pthread_getspecific(Key);
}
```

The implementation of the ONCE class is also straightforward under POSIX — the ONCE class embeds a `pthread_once_t` structure within each ONCE object:

```
typedef void ONCE_FUNCTION(void);

class ONCE {
public:
  ONCE(void);
  ~ONCE(void);
  void Execute(ONCE_FUNCTION*);
private:
  pthread_once_t Flag;
};
```

The ONCE class constructor uses the PTHREAD_ONCE_INIT macro to initialize the Flag field whilst the destructor performs no action:

```
ONCE::ONCE(void) {
  Flag = PTHREAD_ONCE_INIT;
}

ONCE::~ONCE(void) {}
```

The ONCE class Execute() function is easy to implement — it passes the Flag field and a pointer for the once() initialization routine to pthread_once():

```
void ONCE::Execute(ONCE_FUNCTION* once) {
  pthread_once(&Flag,once);
}
```

7.7 Windows Implementation

The Windows operating system provides direct support for keys but one-time initialization has to be implemented indirectly using the 'flag and mutex' technique introduced in section 7.4. The Windows implementation of the KEY class embeds a DWORD key handle within each KEY object:

```
class KEY {
public:
  KEY(void);
  ~KEY(void);
  void Set(void*);
  void* Get(void);
private:
  DWORD Key;
};
```

The KEY class constructor calls the function TlsAlloc() to create a Windows key — the value of the key in all threads is initialized to NULL by TlsAlloc():

```
KEY::KEY(void) {
  Key = TlsAlloc();
}
```

Windows refers to the thread-specific storage facilitated by keys as 'thread local storage' — this explains the 'Tls' prefix appearing in each of the names for key-related Windows functions. The KEY class destructor calls the TlsFree() function to destroy the Windows key created in the constructor:

```
KEY::~KEY(void) {
  TlsFree(Key);
}
```

The KEY class Set() and Get() functions are similarly just wrappers for the Windows TlsSetValue() and TlsGetValue() functions:

```
void KEY::Set(void* value) {
  TlsSetValue(Key,value);
}

void* KEY::Get(void) {
  return TlsGetValue(Key);
}
```

As noted at the start of the section, Windows does not provide direct support for one-time initialization — instead the ONCE class embeds a boolean Flag field in each ONCE object along with a protecting mutex:

```
typedef void ONCE_FUNCTION(void);

class ONCE {
public:
  ONCE(void);
  ~ONCE(void);
  void Execute(ONCE_FUNCTION*);
private:
  BOOL Flag;
  HANDLE Mutex;
};
```

The ONCE class constructor sets the flag to TRUE and creates the mutex — since the ONCE constructor will most likely be executed at program start-up the effect is simply to package the static field declarations from section 7.4 for flag and mutex within a single declaration for a ONCE object.

```
ONCE::ONCE(void) {
  Flag = TRUE;
  Mutex = CreateMutex(NULL,FALSE,NULL);
}
```

The ONCE class destructor just releases the Windows mutex back to the operating system:

```
ONCE::~ONCE(void) {
  CloseHandle(Mutex);
}
```

Finally, the ONCE class Execute() function closely resembles the DEMO class Initialize() function from section 7.4:

```
void ONCE::Execute(ONCE_FUNCTION* once) {
  WaitForSingleObject(Mutex,INFINITE);
  if (Flag) {
    (*once)();
    Flag = FALSE;
  }
  ReleaseMutex(Mutex);
}
```

However, here the one-time initialization is performed by calling the once() function passed in as a parameter by external code.

7.8 Summary

Even though all the threads in a process share the same program code there are many techniques for differentiating the processing performed by the individual threads — perhaps the most obvious method is simply to have different threads execute different pieces of code. When different threads are indeed running the same piece of code one option for specializing their behaviours involves passing parameters to a function that vary according to which thread invokes the function — an alternative is to replace the thread-dependent parameters with thread-specific data referenced through a key. A key is essentially a global pointer whose value is dependent on which thread is currently using the key — the pointer typically references storage allocated in dynamic memory although the thread-specific data may instead be held directly by the key if it can be cast to a **void*** pointer. The KEY class embodies the notion of a key and provides Set() and Get() functions to manipulate the value of the key — immediately after object creation the KEY class Get() function returns NULL until the Set() function is called to explicitly set the KEY object's value. One particularly useful application of the KEY class is to implement thread identifiers for the THREAD class whenever the operating system does not support this functionality directly. A resource which is shared by multiple threads often needs to be initialized only once by a single thread — there are several standard options for achieving such one-time initialization. The easiest approach is to perform the initialization at program start-up using a global declaration statement preferably for either an object or a static class field — the initialization can be fully completed at start-up or alternatively the start-up code can just set a flag that is subsequently examined under mutex protection to determine whether or not the initialization proper is still outstanding. Once program start-up is complete and the main() function has been invoked, the object creation process serves as a good vehicle for implementing one-time initialization — however, thread synchronization may well be necessary to coordinate the creation of an object with the activity of other threads. The ONCE class is specifically designed to facilitate one-time initialization after program start-up — nonetheless, the constructor for a ONCE object is often executed at start-up to provide one-time initialization for the object itself. The ONCE class supplies the Execute() function to execute the desired initialization on behalf of external code — the Execute() function accepts a pointer to an initialization function which is called only by the first thread to successfully invoke Execute(). The ONCE class Execute() function thus provides another example of thread-specific processing — furthermore, the initialization function passed to Execute() may itself behave differently depending on which thread happens to execute it. The KEY and ONCE classes respectively encapsulate the functionality associated with keys and one-time initialization in an operating system independent manner — straightforward implementations of KEY and ONCE classes for both UNIX and Windows operating systems have been described.

8. Multiple Mutexes

It is relatively straightforward to protect a shared resource with a mutex or to signal from one thread to another using an event — however, the complexity of a multi-threaded application increases somewhat when there are several mutexes and events involved. This chapter considers some of the difficulties encountered with multiple mutexes whilst the next chapter looks at the handling of multiple events. A particularly troublesome problem in multi-threaded programming occurs when one or more threads become permanently blocked whilst trying to acquire a set of mutexes — this situation is quite accurately termed 'deadlock'. Probably the most common example of deadlock involves a pair of threads each trying to acquire a resource which is already held by the other. More generally deadlock is possible whenever a 'resource acquisition loop' exists — in this case, each resource in the loop is held by some thread and this thread tries to acquire the next resource in the loop. Fortunately there are a set of standard strategies for overcoming the deadlock problem — unfortunately no one solution covers all possibilities and so some thought is required to choose an effective remedy. For example, a single thread can deadlock itself by trying to reacquire a resource which it already holds — to assist in such circumstances the RECURSIVE_MUTEX class supports the concept of a 'recursive mutex' which allows a thread to successfully make a series of nested Acquire() calls. The main topics covered in this chapter include:

— common causes of deadlock
— resource acquisition diagrams
— methods of avoiding deadlock
— the RECURSIVE_MUTEX class

The chapter concludes by describing the TIMER and CLOCK classes to show some of the deadlock avoidance techniques at work — these classes also illustrate how easily multiple threads allow timing related functionality to be implemented.

8.1 Deadlocking Threads

As an introduction to deadlocking suppose that there are two threads (A and B) which share a pair of resources (X and Y) and that no other threads are involved — resource X is protected by Mutex_X and resource Y is protected by Mutex_Y.

The pair of threads make the following calls to each safely process one of the resources:

thread A	thread B
.	.
`Mutex_X.Acquire();`	`Mutex_Y.Acquire();`
.	.
`// process resource X`	`// process resource Y`
.	.
`Mutex_X.Release();`	`Mutex_Y.Release();`
.	.

Since the threads are acquiring different mutexes the `Acquire()` calls do not block and the threads can immediately continue with their processing of the resources protected by these mutexes. Now suppose that whilst thread A is processing resource X it decides that it also needs to manipulate resource Y — the following sequence of events consequently occurs:

thread A	thread B
.	.
`Mutex_X.Acquire();`	`Mutex_Y.Acquire();`
.	.
`// process resource X`	`// process resource Y`
.	.
.	`Mutex_Y.Release();`
`Mutex_Y.Acquire();`	.
.	.
`// process resources X and Y`	.
.	.
`Mutex_Y.Release();`	.
`Mutex_X.Release();`	.
.	.

When thread A calls `Acquire()` for `Mutex_Y` it is blocked until thread B releases its hold on resource Y by calling the MUTEX object's `Release()` function — when the `Acquire()` call eventually succeeds thread A can complete its processing of resources X and Y before finally releasing the pair of mutexes. Despite the fact that there are actually two MUTEX objects involved this is essentially the same situation as if there were only a single mutex — only `Mutex_Y` plays an active role in the synchronization of threads A and B.

To see how multiple mutexes can really complicate the interaction between the two threads, suppose now that during its processing of resource Y thread B decides to follow the example of thread A and also acquire the other resource (X) — the sequence of calls proceeds as follows:

thread A	thread B
.	.
`Mutex_X.Acquire();`	`Mutex_Y.Acquire();`
.	.
`// process resource X`	`// process resource Y`
.	.
`Mutex_Y.Acquire();`	`Mutex_X.Acquire();`
.	.
.	.
.	.

Now thread A cannot acquire resource Y because thread B already has it and will never release its grasp — similarly, thread B is unable to acquire resource X because thread A will not relinquish its hold on it. The threads are both blocked forever in a deadly embrace — this terminal condition is known as 'deadlock' and is a serious problem for multi-threaded programs. Furthermore, although this example undoubtedly illustrates the most common deadlock scenario there are certainly other possibilities — for example, deadlock will occur whenever a single thread tries to reacquire a resource which can only be acquired once, the result in this case being that the thread blocks forever whilst waiting for the release of a resource which it already holds. The following section discusses a number of approaches for preventing threads from deadlocking — the bad news about deadlock is that there is no general solution to the problem but the good news is that there do exist a variety of standard techniques which can each be applied under a specific set of circumstances.

8.2 Avoiding Deadlock

The most radical solution to avoiding deadlock simply involves reverting to a single-threaded approach — the program is structured so that only one thread uses a particular resource and then, since the resource requires no thread synchronization to protect it, it cannot be the focus of deadlock. Of course, the resource may need to be manipulated as part of the processing performed by several tasks and under normal circumstances each task would be assigned to a separate thread — however, in this context only a single thread is available. Consequently, the lone thread must be used to simulate the activities of multiple threads —

section 1.1 described this technique in detail but the following figure illustrates the basic idea:

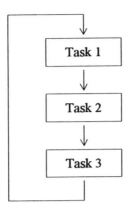

Nonetheless, it is often impractical to structure a program in this manner — after all, multiple threads were introduced precisely to eliminate such convoluted coding methods. If this is indeed the case and multiple threads are involved in manipulating each of the resources causing deadlock then an alternative plan is needed. One possibility is to combine the various resources into a single resource so that there is only one protecting mutex. This is an approach often adopted by pre-existing libraries which are essentially single-threaded — the single library-wide mutex ensures that the code is 'thread-safe' since it cannot be executed by more than one thread at a time. With a single mutex deadlock cannot occur unless there are nested Acquire() calls by the same thread — as noted in section 3.3 the action of trying to reacquire a MUTEX object is undefined and on some operating systems will result in the thread deadlocking. To prevent deadlock from occurring in a portable manner either the inner calls to Acquire() must be removed or else a 'recursive mutex' should be used. One method of removing the inner calls is to pass a flag as a function parameter to indicate whether or not the mutex has already been acquired:

```
void NoDeadlock(int flag) {
  if (flag)
    Mutex.Acquire();
      . . .
        NoDeadlock(FALSE);
      . . .
  if (flag)
    Mutex.Release();
}
```

The top-level call to NoDeadlock() sets the flag to TRUE whilst nested calls set the flag to FALSE — the mutex is thus only acquired and released once.

On the other hand, a recursive mutex guarantees that nested `Acquire()` calls made by the thread which already holds the mutex will always succeed immediately — the following section describes the `RECURSIVE_MUTEX` class that embodies the functionality of a recursive mutex.

If the deadlock problem cannot be side-stepped by having only one thread or by having many threads but only one mutex, then it must be solved by some more subtle means. With two or more resources each protected by a separate mutex the most likely possibility for deadlock is illustrated by the example from the previous section — it is worthwhile examining this example further in order to determine exactly what causes the threads A and B to deadlock. The problem is, in fact, simply that the threads try to acquire the resources X and Y in a different order — if the code is modified as follows then deadlock cannot possibly occur:

thread A	thread B
.	.
`Mutex_X.Acquire();`	.
.	.
`// process resource X`	.
.	.
`Mutex_Y.Acquire();`	.
.	.
`// process resources X and Y`	.
.	.
`Mutex_Y.Release();`	.
`Mutex_X.Release();`	.
.	`Mutex_X.Acquire();`
.	`Mutex_Y.Acquire();`
.	.
.	`// process resources X and Y`
.	.
.	`Mutex_Y.Release();`
.	`Mutex_X.Release();`
.	.

Whenever thread B wants to process resource Y it acquires `Mutex_X` in addition to `Mutex_Y` on the offchance that it will decide to also process resource X. If `Mutex_X` is always acquired before `Mutex_Y` there is no deadlock — to avoid deadlock thread B must acquire `Mutex_X` before `Mutex_Y` just like thread A. However, there is deadlock if thread A acquires `Mutex_X` and then attempts to acquire `Mutex_Y` whilst simultaneously thread B acquires `Mutex_Y` and then attempts to acquire `Mutex_X`. In other words, deadlock occurs because the two threads each try to acquire a resource that has already been acquired by the other.

The following figure illustrates the condition graphically:

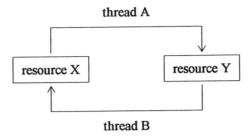

For example, the arrow from resource X to resource Y labelled 'thread A' indicates that whilst thread A is holding resource X it will attempt to acquire resource Y. There is a 'resource acquisition loop' which is characteristic of deadlock — swapping the order in which thread B acquires `Mutex_X` and `Mutex_Y` reverses the direction of one loop segment and so destroys the loop. Finally, note that the order in which threads A and B make their mutex `Release()` calls is not important as far as deadlock is concerned — generally threads should release resources as soon as they have finished using them so as not to delay other threads unnecessarily.

A common technique for ensuring that resources are always acquired in the same order is 'resource layering' — the following figure depicts this technique using a 'resource acquisition diagram':

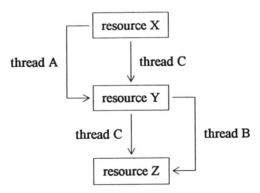

Here there are three layers consisting of the resources X, Y and Z — the layers are stacked one above the other with resource X forming the highest layer and resource Z the lowest. The mutex protecting a higher layer resource is always acquired before the mutex for a lower layer — however, only those resource layers actually needed by a thread must be acquired by that thread. For example, thread A acquires resource X and then resource Y whereas thread B acquires resource Y and then resource Z — thread C acquires all three resources, firstly X then Y and finally Z. Since the resource acquisitions always occur from top to bottom there can be no loops and so deadlock will not occur.

Sometimes resource layering almost solves the deadlock problem but not quite —
the threads involved acquire the layered resources in the correct order most of the
time but occasionally a thread must acquire a mutex for a higher layer resource
after a lower layer one. Considering the deadlock example from the previous
section, suppose that most threads act like thread A and acquire resource X before
resource Y — however, thread B is resolutely determined to acquire resource Y
before resource X. In this case it may be possible to avoid deadlock by having
thread B attempt to acquire `Mutex_X` with a call to its `Acquired()` function —
if resource X is already held then thread B temporarily abandons its processing of
the resource and tries again later:

```
int done = FALSE;
while (!done) {
  Mutex_Y.Acquire();
    .
  // pre-process resource Y
    .
  if (Mutex_X.Acquired()) {
      .
    // process resource X
      .
    Mutex_X.Release();
    done = TRUE;
  }
    .
  // post-process resource Y
    .
  Mutex_Y.Release();
  if (!done)
    Sleep(10);
}
```

Here thread B continually loops, sleeping for a short time between each attempt,
until it manages to process resource X — a disadvantage of this technique is that
there is no guarantee that thread B will ever manage to acquire resource X. At the
start of the loop there is some preparatory processing of resource Y in anticipation
that resource X actually will be acquired — depending whether the `Acquired()`
call succeeds or not the code at the end of the loop can undo any changes made to
resource Y or alternatively it can perform additional processing of resource Y
before the loop exits. The TIMER class described in section 8.4 provides a more
complete example of this technique for avoiding deadlock. In general the solution
applies whenever one set of threads acquire resource X and then resource Y whilst
another set acquire the resources in the reverse order. An alternative approach in

such a situation is to split one of the resources (Y) into two resources (Y and Z) so that the resource acquisition loop is broken — the following figure illustrates this approach:

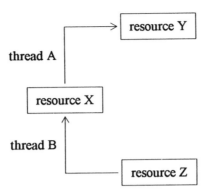

Threads like thread A acquire resource X and then resource Y whilst threads like thread B acquire resource Z and then resource X:

thread A   **thread B**

      .   .

```
Mutex_X.Acquire();        Mutex_Z.Acquire();
```
      .   .

```
// process resource X     // process resource Z
```
      .   .

```
Mutex_Y.Acquire();
```
      .   .

```
// process resources X and Y
```
      .   .

```
Mutex_Y.Release();
Mutex_X.Release();
```
      .   `Mutex_X.Acquire();`

      .   .

      .   `// process resources Z and X`

      .   .

      .   `Mutex_X.Release();`

      .   `Mutex_Z.Release();`

      .   .

In some situations it may be possible to combine the various techniques previously described — however, care is needed to ensure that the combination really does cure the deadlock problem. For instance, continuing the previous example, suppose

that there is a third set of threads (represented by thread C) which do not need
resource X at all and use the resource layering approach for acquiring resources Y
and Z — the following figure illustrates the relevant resource acquisitions:

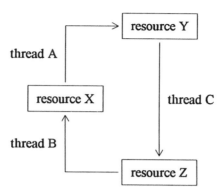

Now there is a loop from resource X to resource Y, from resource Y to resource Z
and from resource Z back to resource X — the presence of this resource acquisition
loop again opens up the possibility of deadlock:

thread A	**thread B**	**thread C**
.	.	.
Mutex_X.Acquire();	.	.
.	Mutex_Z.Acquire();	.
.	.	Mutex_Y.Acquire();
.	.	.
Mutex_Y.Acquire();	.	.
.	Mutex_X.Acquire();	.
.	.	Mutex_Z.Acquire();
.	.	.

Most deadlock avoidance techniques described in this section rely on the fact that
deadlock depends on different threads acquiring resources in a different order — it
is reasonable to wonder, therefore, whether deadlock could be avoided if threads
were to acquire all the mutexes they require simultaneously since this would
remove any question about the order of acquisition. It is certainly possible to
convert the acquisition of multiple mutexes into a single atomic operation — a
thread blocks until all mutexes it wants are available and then it acquires all the
mutexes together. However, this assumes that a thread acquires its mutexes at one
point in the program with no intervening code between the acquisitions — either
this is true everywhere or else somewhere the mutexes are acquired with other code
intermingled and then there must be some safe order of mutex acquisition if
deadlock is impossible. In any case whenever several Acquire() calls do occur

together it is unnecessary to acquire the mutexes simultaneously and instead the function calls can simply be arranged in an order that prevents deadlock. However, the same cannot be said whenever both mutexes and events are concerned — the simplest scenario involves waiting for an event to be signalled and then atomically acquiring a mutex whenever the signal is received. The second attempt at implementing the SYNCH class in section 5.8 nicely illustrates the situation — in this case the mutex and the event of interest are provided by the MUTEX object and the EVENT object embedded within a SYNCH object. The SYNCH class Broadcast() function sets the event to signal to any waiting threads that the synchronization state of the SYNCH object has changed significantly:

```
void SYNCH::Broadcast(void* context) {
  WaitForSingleObject(Mutex,INFINITE);
  if (Update(context) && Waiters) {
    Runners += Waiters;
    Waiters = 0;
    SetEvent(Event);
  }
  ReleaseMutex(Mutex);
}
```

When a thread has decided to wait in the SYNCH class Wait() function, it must wait for the EVENT object and acquire the MUTEX object. The mutex cannot be acquired first or else Broadcast() will never be able to set the event in the first place — so suppose the thread waits for the event before the mutex is acquired:

```
int SYNCH::Wait(void* context) {
  int status;
  do {
    WaitForSingleObject(Mutex,INFINITE);
    status = Status(context);
    if (status == SYNCH_WAIT)
      Waiters++;
    ReleaseMutex(Mutex);
    if (status == SYNCH_WAIT) {
      WaitForSingleObject(Event,INFINITE);
      WaitForSingleObject(Mutex,INFINITE);
      if (--Runners)
        SetEvent(Event);
      ReleaseMutex(Mutex);
    }
  } while (status == SYNCH_WAIT);
  return (status == SYNCH_OKAY);
}
```

With this implementation of the SYNCH class Broadcast() and Wait() functions the following sequence of events is possible:

thread A	thread B	thread C
.	.	.
.	Waiters = 1	.
Waiters = 0	.	.
Runners = 1	.	.
set event in Broadcast()	.	.
.	.	Waiters = 1
.	reset event in Wait()	.
Waiters = 0	.	.
Runners = 2	.	.
set event in Broadcast()	.	.
.	.	reset event in Wait()
.	Runners = 1	.
.	set event in Wait()	.
.	.	Runners = 0
.	.	.

Now since both threads B and C have escaped from the Wait() function there are no 'runners' but nonetheless the event is still set — this happened because the Broadcast() function was able to signal to thread C before the Wait() function had finished processing the signal to thread B. Waiting for the event and acquiring the mutex atomically will prevent this interference from occurring:

thread A	thread B	thread C
.	.	.
.	Waiters = 1	.
Waiters = 0	.	.
Runners = 1	.	.
set event in Broadcast()	.	.
.	.	Waiters = 1
.	reset event in Wait()	.
.	Runners = 0	.
Waiters = 0	.	.
Runners = 1	.	.
set event in Broadcast()	.	.
.	.	reset event in Wait()
.	.	Runners = 0
.	.	.

The final implementation of the SYNCH class described in section 5.8 actually sidesteps the problem altogether. Nonetheless the SYNCH class Wait() function packages the code needed to wait on an event and acquire a mutex as a single atomic operation and so deriving a custom synchronization class from the SYNCH base class is probably the simplest option available whenever such functionality is required. Indeed a related application of derived synchronization classes involving multiple events appears in the MULTI_EVENT class implementation of section 9.6.

8.3 The RECURSIVE_MUTEX Class

As noted in section 3.3 the action of a thread trying to reacquire a MUTEX object which it already holds is undefined — depending on the operating system it may cause the thread to deadlock. The RECURSIVE_MUTEX class is derived from the MUTEX class specifically to allow a thread to reacquire a mutex — once the thread has acquired a RECURSIVE_MUTEX object any nested Acquire() calls it makes for the same object are guaranteed to succeed immediately. In other respects a RECURSIVE_MUTEX object acts just as though it were a MUTEX object — however, the implementation of a MUTEX object is typically more efficient and so a MUTEX object should be used in preference to a RECURSIVE_MUTEX object unless the additional functionality of the latter is particularly needed.

```
recursive_mutex.h:

#ifndef _RECURSIVE_MUTEX_HEADER
#define _RECURSIVE_MUTEX_HEADER
#include "os.h"
#include "synch.h"
#include "mutex.h"

class RECURSIVE_MUTEX_SYNCH : public SYNCH {
public:
  RECURSIVE_MUTEX_SYNCH(void);
  ~RECURSIVE_MUTEX_SYNCH(void);
protected:
  virtual int Status(void* = NULL);
  virtual int Update(void* = NULL);
private:
  unsigned int ThreadID;
  int Count;
};

class RECURSIVE_MUTEX : public MUTEX {
    ...
private:
  RECURSIVE_MUTEX_SYNCH Synch;
};

#endif
```

This implementation of the RECURSIVE_MUTEX class is made independent of the underlying operating system by building on the services of the SYNCH class — each RECURSIVE_MUTEX object embeds an object from the custom synchronization class RECURSIVE_MUTEX_SYNCH which derives from the SYNCH base class. A RECURSIVE_MUTEX object works by recording the identifier of the thread currently holding the mutex in the ThreadID field — the Count field is used to count the number of times this thread has successfully called either Acquire() or Acquired() without yet making a matching call to the Release() function. Each successful call a thread makes to either of the RECURSIVE_MUTEX class functions Acquire() or Acquired() must be matched with a call to the RECURSIVE_MUTEX class Release() function — this function decrements the Count field and only releases the mutex whenever the count returns to zero. The RECURSIVE_MUTEX_SYNCH class constructor resets the Count field to zero whilst the destructor performs no processing:

```
recursive_mutex.cxx:

#include "thread.h"
#include "synch.h"
#include "recursive_mutex.h"

RECURSIVE_MUTEX_SYNCH::RECURSIVE_MUTEX_SYNCH(void) {
  Count = 0;
}


RECURSIVE_MUTEX_SYNCH::~RECURSIVE_MUTEX_SYNCH(void) {}
```

The RECURSIVE_MUTEX class Acquire() and Acquired() functions both call the Wait() function of the embedded RECURSIVE_MUTEX_SYNCH object and this then invokes the derived class version of the Status() function:

```
int RECURSIVE_MUTEX_SYNCH::Status(void* non_blocking) {
  int status = SYNCH_WAIT;
  unsigned int thread_id = THREAD::GetCurrentThreadID();
  if (Count == 0) {
    Count++;
    ThreadID = thread_id;
    status = SYNCH_OKAY;
  }
  else if (ThreadID == thread_id) {
    Count++;
    status = SYNCH_OKAY;
  }
  else if (non_blocking)
    status = SYNCH_FAIL;
  return status;
}
```

If the Count field is zero when the Status() function is executed then the mutex is being freshly acquired by a new thread and the thread identifier is stored in the ThreadID field — otherwise the mutex has already been acquired and so the Status() function must check the current thread ID against that of the current owner to determine whether or not the mutex acquisition attempt will succeed. The RECURSIVE_MUTEX class Acquire() function passes in a NULL value for the non_blocking parameter whilst the Acquired() function passes in a non-NULL value — if the acquisition fails then the Acquire() function will block until it can succeed whereas the Acquired() function will return a FALSE status value immediately. The RECURSIVE_MUTEX class Release() function calls the Signal() function of the embedded RECURSIVE_MUTEX_SYNCH object and this invokes the derived class Update() function:

```
int RECURSIVE_MUTEX_SYNCH::Update(void*) {
  return (--Count == 0);
}
```

The RECURSIVE_MUTEX_SYNCH class Update() function decrements the Count field and indicates that a signal be sent to a thread waiting to acquire the mutex only if the count has returned to zero. This completes the definition of the RECURSIVE_MUTEX_SYNCH class — with a RECURSIVE_MUTEX_SYNCH object embedded within each RECURSIVE_MUTEX object the implementation of the RECURSIVE_MUTEX class is trivial:

```
class RECURSIVE_MUTEX : public MUTEX {
public:
  RECURSIVE_MUTEX(void);
  virtual ~RECURSIVE_MUTEX(void);
  virtual void Acquire(void);
  virtual int Acquired(void);
  virtual void Release(void);
private:
  RECURSIVE_MUTEX_SYNCH Synch;
};
```

The RECURSIVE_MUTEX class constructor and destructor both do nothing:

```
RECURSIVE_MUTEX::RECURSIVE_MUTEX(void) {}

RECURSIVE_MUTEX::~RECURSIVE_MUTEX(void) {}
```

The RECURSIVE_MUTEX class Acquire() function just calls the embedded Synch object's Wait() function implicitly passing the default NULL parameter to indicate that Wait() should block if the mutex cannot be acquired immediately:

```
void RECURSIVE_MUTEX::Acquire(void) {
  Synch.Wait();
}
```

The RECURSIVE_MUTEX class Acquired() function similarly calls the embedded object's Wait() function but this time the non_blocking parameter is not NULL — the Acquired() function will consequently return FALSE immediately if it is unable to acquire the mutex.

```
int RECURSIVE_MUTEX::Acquired(void) {
  int non_blocking;
  return Synch.Wait(&non_blocking);
}
```

Finally, the RECURSIVE_MUTEX class Release() function simply calls the Synch object's Signal() function:

```
void RECURSIVE_MUTEX::Release(void) {
  Synch.Signal();
}
```

As previously noted each successful call to Acquire() or Acquired() must be matched by a corresponding call to Release():

```
void NoDeadlock(RECURSIVE_MUTEX* mutex) {
  mutex->Acquire();
      ...
  mutex->Release();
}

RECURSIVE_MUTEX mutex;
if (mutex.Acquired()) {
    ...
  NoDeadlock(&mutex);
    ...
  mutex.Release();
}
```

The mutex is only actually released after the final Release() call. A fuller example illustrating the use of a RECURSIVE_MUTEX object is provided by the TIMER class described in the next section.

8.4 The TIMER Class

This section describes the TIMER class to illustrate some of the points about working with mutexes made in earlier sections of the chapter — the next section describes the CLOCK class to complete the example. The TIMER class provides a convenient mechanism for scheduling activities which must occur at some point in the future — an activity is scheduled by calling the Schedule() function of a TIMER object:

```
TIMER timer;
timer.Schedule(&activity,delay);
```

The `Schedule()` function must also be passed the delay desired before the activity is triggered — the delay value is specified in 'ticks' with one tick being nominally equivalent to a tenth of a second although the actual delay will increase as the processing load on the system rises. Just as the actions forming an atomic operation (see section 3.6) are specified using the `ATOMIC_ACTION` interface class so a timer activity is specified using the `TIMER_ACTIVITY` interface class — the first parameter passed to the `TIMER` class `Schedule()` function is a `TIMER_ACTIVITY*` pointer. The `TIMER_ACTIVITY` class includes a single function in the timer activity interface:

```
class TIMER_ACTIVITY {
public:
  virtual void Trigger(void) = 0;
};
```

An activity is actually defined by deriving an activity class from the `TIMER_ACTIVITY` interface class and implementing the `Trigger()` function in the derived class — once the activity has been scheduled the `TIMER` object involved will invoke the `Trigger()` function after the requested delay. A single timer can be used to schedule several activities:

```
TIMER timer;
int identifier_A =
      timer.Schedule(&activity_A,delay_A);
int identifier_B =
      timer.Schedule(&activity_B,delay_B);
```

The `Schedule()` function returns an activity ID which can be used to cancel the activity before it is triggered — the identifier must be passed to the `TIMER` object's `Cancel()` function to request the cancellation. For example:

```
timer.Cancel(identifier_A);
```

However, it is important not to pass an identifier to the `Cancel()` function which corresponds to an activity that has already been triggered — as soon as the `Trigger()` function for the activity has been executed the identifier may be reassigned to a new activity. The problem can be easily avoided by resetting the variable holding the activity identifier to an invalid value (-1) within the `Trigger()` function — for example:

```
void DEMO_ACTIVITY::Trigger(void) {
   ...
   ActivityID = -1;
}
```

The `CLOCK` class from the following section also illustrates this requirement.

Finally, the TIMER class Schedule() function allows a MUTEX object to be passed as an optional third parameter — when the TIMER object executes an activity it will acquire the associated mutex for the duration of the Trigger() function.

The full specification for the TIMER class is as follows:

```
const TIMER_MAX_ACTIVITIES = 100;

class TIMER : public THREAD {
public:
    TIMER(void);
    ~TIMER(void);
    int Schedule(TIMER_ACTIVITY*,int,MUTEX* = NULL);
    void Cancel(int);
protected:
    virtual void* Run(void*);
private:
    TIMER_ACTIVITY* Activities[TIMER_MAX_ACTIVITIES];
    MUTEX* Mutexes[TIMER_MAX_ACTIVITIES];
    int Delays[TIMER_MAX_ACTIVITIES];
    RECURSIVE_MUTEX Mutex;
    EVENT Quit;
};
```

The 'activity-delay-mutex' triples passed to the TIMER class Schedule() function are stored in the three arrays Activities, Delays and Mutexes — the TIMER class constructor initializes the Activities array with NULL values to indicate that there are initially no activities scheduled:

```
TIMER::TIMER(void) {
    for (int i=0; (i<TIMER_MAX_ACTIVITIES); i++)
        Activities[i] = (TIMER_ACTIVITY*)NULL;
    Start();
}
```

The constructor also starts the thread inherited from the THREAD base class by calling the Start() function — the thread loops endlessly until it is signalled to stop by the TIMER class destructor:

```
TIMER::~TIMER(void) {
    Quit.Signal();
    Wait();
}
```

The `Activities`, `Mutexes` and `Delays` arrays are updated by the TIMER class `Schedule()` function whenever a new activity is scheduled:

```
int TIMER::Schedule(TIMER_ACTIVITY* activity,
                    int delay, MUTEX* mutex) {
  int i;
  Mutex.Acquire();
  for (i=0; (i<TIMER_MAX_ACTIVITIES); i++)
    if (Activities[i] == NULL)
      break;
  if (i < TIMER_MAX_ACTIVITIES) {
    Activities[i] = activity;
    Mutexes[i] = mutex;
    Delays[i] = delay;
  }
  else
    i = -1;
  Mutex.Release();
  return i;
}
```

The arrays are manipulated under the protection of the MUTEX object which is embedded within the TIMER object — this mutex must be recursive because it is held by the TIMER object's internal thread as it calls the various activity `Trigger()` functions and the activity code is free to call the TIMER class `Schedule()` function if, for example, it is desired to set up an activity which is triggered at regular intervals. The TIMER class `Schedule()` function simply scans through the `Activities` array looking for a free slot. If one is found then the `Activities`, `Mutexes` and `Delays` arrays are updated using the three parameters passed to the `Schedule()` function and the position in the arrays where the triple is stored is returned as the activity ID — otherwise the `Schedule()` function returns the invalid identifier value -1 to indicate that the activity has not been successfully scheduled. The TIMER class `Cancel()` function simply checks that the activity identifier passed as a parameter is within bounds and then sets the appropriate element of the `Activities` array to NULL:

```
void TIMER::Cancel(int i) {
  Mutex.Acquire();
  if ((i>=0) && (i<TIMER_MAX_ACTIVITIES))
    Activities[i] = (TIMER_ACTIVITY*)NULL;
  Mutex.Release();
}
```

As previously noted the caller of the `Cancel()` function is responsible for ensuring that an out-of-date activity identifier is not passed as a parameter.

The internal thread run by the TIMER object takes responsibility for triggering activities as it executes the TIMER class Run() function:

```
void* TIMER::Run(void*) {
  int i;
  while (!Quit.Test()) {
    Mutex.Acquire();
    for (i=0; (i<TIMER_MAX_ACTIVITIES); i++)
      if (Activities[i])
        if (Delays[i] <= 0) {
          if (Mutexes[i] == NULL)
            Activities[i]->Trigger();
          else if (Mutexes[i]->Acquired()) {
            Activities[i]->Trigger();
            Mutexes[i]->Release();
          }
          Activities[i] = (TIMER_ACTIVITY*)NULL;
        }
        else
          Delays[i]--;
    Mutex.Release();
    Sleep(100);
  }
  return NULL;
}
```

The Run() function loops repeatedly, sleeping for a tenth of a second between attempts to trigger scheduled activities — the loop finally terminates whenever the TIMER class destructor signals the Quit event. On each iteration of the loop the internal TIMER thread looks through the Activities array for values that are not NULL and whenever one is found the corresponding delay value in the Delays array is decremented — if the delay has reached zero then the activity is triggered by calling its Trigger() function through the TIMER_ACTIVITY* pointer. If the activity has an associated mutex then its Acquired() function is invoked prior to executing the Trigger() function for the activity. The TIMER class must assume that the mutex associated with an activity may be held by external code whilst that code is calling either of the TIMER class Schedule() or Cancel() functions — thus the normal order of mutex acquisition is firstly an activity mutex and then the TIMER object mutex. However, the TIMER class Run() function acquires the TIMER object mutex before the activity mutexes — as explained in section 8.2 in order to avoid deadlock it is important not to call the blocking Acquire() function to acquire the activity mutexes. Furthermore, even putting aside the question of deadlock, using the non-blocking Acquired() function ensures that the internal TIMER thread is not held up unduly whenever an activity mutex is held by external code — this helps to maintain the accuracy of the delays requested by the other scheduled activities. Similarly, the various activity `Trigger()` functions must execute within a reasonable amount of time if the `TIMER` object is to operate reliably.

8.5 The `CLOCK` Class

This section describes the `CLOCK` class that makes use of the services provided by the `TIMER` class introduced in the previous section — the same points about working with mutexes are discussed again but from a different perspective. The `CLOCK` class defines its timer activity by deriving the `CLOCK_TICK` class from the `TIMER_ACTIVITY` interface class — the `CLOCK_TICK` class implements its `Trigger()` function so that it provides the 'tick' for an associated `CLOCK` object. The full specification for the `CLOCK_TICK` class is as follows:

```
class CLOCK;

class CLOCK_TICK : public TIMER_ACTIVITY {
public:
  CLOCK_TICK(CLOCK*);
  ~CLOCK_TICK(void);
  virtual void Trigger(void);
private:
  CLOCK* Clock;
};
```

The `CLOCK_TICK` class constructor is passed a pointer to the associated `CLOCK` object and this is stored in the `Clock` field of the `CLOCK_TICK` object — the `CLOCK_TICK` class destructor performs no processing:

```
CLOCK_TICK::CLOCK_TICK(CLOCK* clock) {
  Clock = clock;
}

CLOCK_TICK::~CLOCK_TICK(void) {}
```

Each time the `TIMER` object calls the `CLOCK_TICK` class `Trigger()` function the `Tick()` function of the associated `CLOCK` object is invoked:

```
void CLOCK_TICK::Trigger(void) {
  Clock->Tick();
}
```

The `CLOCK` class `Tick()` function is a private function to prevent external code from calling it and so the `CLOCK_TICK` class must be made into a friend class of the `CLOCK` class.

The CLOCK class has the following specification:

```
class CLOCK {
friend class CLOCK_TICK;
public:
  CLOCK(void);
  ~CLOCK(void);
  void SetTime(int,int,int);
  void GetTime(int&,int&,int&);
  void Zero(void);
  void Go(void);
  void Halt(void);
private:
  void Tick(void);
  static TIMER Timer;
  CLOCK_TICK* Ticker;
  int TickerID;
  int Time;
  MUTEX Mutex;
};
```

The CLOCK class has a TIMER object embedded as a static field — this timer is shared by all the CLOCK objects. However, each CLOCK object has its own CLOCK_TICK object which calls that particular CLOCK object's Tick() function — there is also a TickerID field for each CLOCK object so that the individual activities scheduled using the shared timer can be referenced. The CLOCK class constructor initializes the CLOCK object's associated CLOCK_TICK object by passing it a pointer to the CLOCK object — the CLOCK class TickerID field is initialized to the invalid activity identifier −1 to indicate that no CLOCK_TICK activity is currently scheduled:

```
CLOCK::CLOCK(void) {
  Ticker = new CLOCK_TICK(this);
  TickerID = -1;
  Time = 0;
}
```

The CLOCK class constructor also sets the Time field — this field is incremented each time that the CLOCK object's Tick() function is invoked. The clock ticks are started by calling the CLOCK class Go() function:

```
void CLOCK::Go(void) {
  Mutex.Acquire();
  if (TickerID == -1)
    TickerID = Timer.Schedule(Ticker,10,&Mutex);
  Mutex.Release();
}
```

The Go() function checks the TickerID field to determine whether the CLOCK object is already ticking and if it is not then a CLOCK_TICK activity is scheduled by calling the shared TIMER object's Schedule() function with a nominal delay of one second. Note that the MUTEX object associated with the CLOCK_TICK activity is also used by the CLOCK object to protect its own internal data — since the TIMER class Schedule() function is not called if the CLOCK_TICK activity is currently scheduled then the Go() function cannot possibly cause the TIMER class Run() function to deadlock whenever it tries to acquire the activity mutex. However, the same is not true of the CLOCK class Halt() function which must be called to stop the clock from ticking:

```
void CLOCK::Halt(void) {
  Mutex.Acquire();
  if (TickerID != -1) {
    Timer.Cancel(TickerID);
    TickerID = -1;
  }
  Mutex.Release();
}
```

The Halt() function only calls the TIMER class Cancel() function if there actually is a scheduled activity to cancel — after the Cancel() call there is no longer a CLOCK_TICK activity scheduled and so the TickerID field is invalidated by setting it to -1. During the time that Halt() is calling Cancel() the TIMER class Run() function could decide to trigger the activity — the deadlock avoidance strategy used by Run() to acquire the activity mutex is essential in this instance. If the CLOCK object is still ticking whenever it is destroyed then the CLOCK class destructor calls Halt() to prevent the shared CLOCK class TIMER object from triggering an activity for a non-existent CLOCK object:

```
CLOCK::~CLOCK(void) {
  Halt();
  delete Ticker;
}
```

Whenever a CLOCK_TICK activity is indeed triggered the CLOCK_TICK class Trigger() function calls the CLOCK class Tick() function — the Tick() function increments the Time field and schedules another CLOCK_TICK activity for the next second:

```
void CLOCK::Tick(void) {
  if (++Time == CLOCK_DAY)
    Time = 0;
  TickerID = Timer.Schedule(Ticker,10,&Mutex);
}
```

The Time field wraps back to zero at the end of the day — the CLOCK_DAY constant holds the number of seconds in one day:

```
const int CLOCK_DAY = 24*60*60;
```

The TIMER class Schedule() function is called inside Tick() — Tick() is called by Trigger() which is called by Run() and all the while the TIMER object's internal mutex is held. Since the Schedule() function always acquires this same mutex when it is invoked it is clear that the mutex must be recursive in order to guarantee that deadlock will not occur — indeed the internal TIMER mutex is provided by the RECURSIVE_MUTEX class. The CLOCK class Tick() function also updates the TickerID field so that it refers to the currently scheduled activity — this is important whenever Halt() invokes the TIMER class Cancel() function. The CLOCK class SetTime() function allows the Time field to be set to an arbitrary time-of-day value so that the CLOCK object can be used as an ordinary clock:

```
void CLOCK::SetTime(int hour,int minute,int second) {
  Mutex.Acquire();
  Time = 60*(60*hour+minute)+second;
  Mutex.Release();
}
```

Alternatively, the convenience function Zero() is available to zero the Time field whenever the CLOCK object is used as a stop-watch:

```
void CLOCK::Zero(void) {
  SetTime(0,0,0);
}
```

The current time held by a CLOCK object can be retrieved by calling the CLOCK class GetTime() function:

```
void CLOCK::GetTime(int& hour,int& minute,int& second)
{
  Mutex.Acquire();
  hour = Time/3600;
  minute = (Time/60)%60;
  second = Time%60;
  Mutex.Release();
}
```

As explained for the GetName() function of section 3.5, the GetTime() function cannot in general be replaced by three separate functions GetHour(), GetMinute() and GetSecond() since the Time field may well change between individual calls to these functions.

The following code sample illustrates a typical application of the CLOCK class —
a CLOCK object repeatedly times how long it takes the user to perform some
activity:

```
CLOCK clock;
for (int i=0; (i<10); i++) {
  clock.Zero();
  clock.Go();
  printf("Count to 1000 and hit ENTER\n");
  getchar();
  clock.Halt();
  clock.GetTime(hour,minute,second);
  printf("That took %i hours %i minutes %i seconds\n",
                  hour, minute, second);
}
```

8.6 Summary

This chapter has been principally concerned with deadlock and the means of
avoiding it. The most common example of deadlock occurs when a pair of threads
each try to acquire a resource that is already held by the other — another possibility
is that a single thread attempts to reacquire a resource which it already holds. More
generally deadlock is possible if a loop exists in the resource acquisition diagram
for the program — deadlock actually does occur when every resource in the loop is
held by some thread and this thread tries to acquire the next resource in the loop.
Most techniques for avoiding deadlock rely on breaking a resource acquisition loop
in some manner — for example, one segment of the loop may be reversed by
acquiring the corresponding pair of resources in the opposite order or alternatively
one resource in the loop may be split into two so that a gap in the loop is created.
Another option which prevents the formation of a loop in the first place is to adopt
the resource layering principle — this demands that threads must always acquire
higher layer resources before lower layer ones so that a resource acquisition loop is
impossible. A variation on the standard resource layering approach is to identify
exceptional cases where a higher layer resource must be acquired after lower layer
ones and to attempt the acquisition of the higher layer resource using the
non-blocking MUTEX class Acquired() function — if the call is unsuccessful
then the lower layer resources must be released and the whole procedure repeated
later. Aside from emulating multi-tasking with a single thread in order to permit
the removal of all mutex synchronization, the most basic solution to deadlock is to
combine the relevant resources into one and then rely on a single mutex — even in
this situation deadlock is still possible unless all nested Acquire() calls are
removed or else made harmless through the use of a recursive mutex. The
RECURSIVE_MUTEX class embodies the functionality of a recursive mutex —
nested calls by the same thread to reacquire a recursive mutex are guaranteed to
succeed immediately. The RECURSIVE_MUTEX class builds on the services of the
SYNCH class and can thus be implemented in a manner independent of the
underlying operating system. Each RECURSIVE_MUTEX object embeds a custom

synchronization object that performs the bulk of the work — the embedded object records the ID of the thread currently holding the mutex and also maintains a mutex acquisition count. The acquisition count is incremented by each successful call to `Acquire()` or `Acquired()` and is decremented by matching calls to `Release()` — the holding thread actually releases the mutex only when the count is returned to zero. The `TIMER` class is designed to enable various activities to be scheduled for execution at some point in the future — an activity is defined by deriving an activity class from the `TIMER_ACTIVITY` interface class and overriding the requisite `Trigger()` function. The `TIMER` class `Schedule()` function accepts an 'activity-delay-mutex' triple — the delay desired before the activity is triggered is specified in 'ticks' (nominally tenths of a second) and the mutex will be acquired internally by the `TIMER` object to provide protection for the duration of the `Trigger()` callback. The `Schedule()` function returns an activity ID which can be passed to the `TIMER` class `Cancel()` function in order to cancel an activity before it is triggered — the `CLOCK` class illustrates the requirement that the activity ID handle must be invalidated within the `Trigger()` function or whenever the activity is cancelled. The `TIMER` and `CLOCK` classes demonstrate two deadlock avoidance techniques — firstly, the internal `TIMER` mutex is recursive to accommodate the case where `Schedule()` is called within `Trigger()` and secondly, repeated attempts to acquire the activity mutexes in a non-blocking manner are used lest these mutexes are already held by external code which is currently calling the `Schedule()` or `Cancel()` functions. Finally, custom synchronization classes typically provide the simplest way to manage the process of waiting for an event and then atomically acquiring a mutex whenever the event signal is received — the code to implement this functionality is neatly packaged within the `SYNCH` base class. Indeed custom synchronization classes can often be applied effectively in other similar situations involving multiple mutexes and events — for example, the `MULTI_EVENT` class described in the next chapter allows a thread to wait for one or all events in some pre-defined set to become signalled simultaneously.

9. Multiple Events

Avoiding deadlock is the principal concern involved when working with multiple mutexes — however, this is typically less of a problem for multiple events where the prime difficulty is usually accommodating the unpredictable order in which different events may occur. There are basically two common modes of operation — either a thread can wait for one out of several events to be signalled or alternatively the thread can wait for all events in a set to become signalled simultaneously. In the latter case several threads may be waiting for some of the same events so that the various event sets overlap — to prevent holding up other threads unnecessarily a thread must only receive a signal for one of the events it is waiting for if it can do so for all such events together. The MULTI_EVENT class is designed to support both of these modes of operation — each MULTI_EVENT object manages a collection of events internally and each of these events may be referenced using a unique integer 'cookie' value. The key topics covered by this chapter include:

— overlapping event sets
— random event monitoring
— the MULTI_EVENT class
— implementation details for UNIX and Windows

The chapter also updates the Hello program from chapter 2 in order to illustrate the use of multiple events in a sizeable example — for added interest the updated version incorporates some of the multi-threading techniques introduced throughout the intervening chapters.

9.1 Multiple Events

Multiple events are typically utilized in situations where the exact order in which the various events are signalled is unpredictable — the following two uses of multiple events commonly arise in real applications:

1. random event monitoring
2. overlapping event sets

The first case applies whenever a single thread must wait for one of several different events to occur — the thread has no idea which event will happen first but

must monitor them all simultaneously. A common activity which nicely illustrates
the basic concept of 'random event monitoring' is input/output processing since in
this situation the time taken to complete a particular read or write operation is, in
general, beyond the control of the program — the input/output thread might
schedule a number of reads or writes and then wait for individual events to
signal the completion of the various requests. In fact, the UNIX operating system
supplies the `select()` function to help applications manage multiple input/output
operations concurrently and the Windows operating system similarly supports
'asynchronous input/output' — however, a less specific solution is needed to permit
monitoring of random events in a more general context. A lone monitoring thread
could poll a set of EVENT objects by repeatedly calling their `Test()` function but
this is not a very efficient option — alternatively the single thread could be
replaced with multiple threads each monitoring its own event in a blocking manner
but this rather sidesteps the issue and the interactions between the various threads
will probably still need to be coordinated. Fortunately, the MULTI_EVENT class
described in the next section is designed expressly to allow a single thread to
monitor multiple events in a straightforward manner.

The MULTI_EVENT class is also useful when 'overlapping event sets' are involved
— an 'event set' is simply a collection of events that must be signalled
simultaneously before a particular thread can proceed and the sets overlap if several
threads must wait for events common to different sets. The following figure
illustrates a basic example of overlapping event sets:

Here thread A requires events X and Z whereas thread B needs events Y and Z —
both threads must wait for event Z and the event sets overlap. If ordinary EVENT
objects are used then the problems arise whenever event Z is signalled — it is not
clear whether the event should be passed to thread A or to thread B. If thread A
accepts the signal and then event Y is signalled, thread B will be unable to continue
even though both events it waits for have occurred — similarly if thread B takes the
signal and then event X occurs, thread A will be held up unnecessarily. In the
worst case a wrong decision may lead to deadlock — for example, suppose that
thread C periodically signals event Z to alternately release thread A or thread B
with the choice of thread being dictated by the current states of events X and Y.

This situation is illustrated by the following code snippets:

```
        thread A                thread B                thread C

            .                       .                       .
            .                       .           // signal event X
while (...) {            while (...) {           while (...) {
            .                       .           // signal event Z
    // await events         // await events             .
    //   X and Z            //   Y and Z                .
    t = "Tick";             t = "Tock";                 .
    // signal events        // signal events            .
    //   Y and W            //   X and W                .
            .                       .           // await event W
            .                       .           printf("%s\n",t);
}                       }                       }
```

In correct operation thread A firstly waits for events X and Z before signalling event Y, then thread B waits for events Y and Z before signalling event X and so on — whenever either thread A or thread B finishes its processing it also signals event W to allow thread C to send out the next rhythmic signal to event Z. The overall arrangement is a variation on the basic 'producer-consumer' paradigm of sections 4.3 and 4.4 but with the role of producer alternating back and forth between threads A and B. Now suppose that there is a malfunction of the intended design and initially thread B intercepts the signal to event Z before thread A ever realizes that both events X and Z have been signalled. In this situation, all three threads A, B and C will block indefinitely each waiting for a different event to be signalled — thread A waits for event Z, thread B waits for event Y and thread C waits for event W. Of course, this is a rather contrived example and the problem could easily be avoided by ensuring threads A and B wait for their respective events X and Y before event Z — nonetheless, this solution does introduce a specific ordering in which to wait for multiple events and as the previous chapter has shown such ordering is a good way to encourage deadlock. The next section describes the example again under the guise of the TICK_TOCK class and also discusses how to safely wait for the multiple events in an event set using a MULTI_EVENT object. Indeed the MULTI_EVENT class can be useful in a variety of related situations that involve both events and mutexes — as discussed in section 4.1, apart from the ability of a mutex to be held by a particular thread, the two synchronization primitive types (events and mutexes) are very similar and so an event can be used to simulate a mutex. For example, the 'event-and-mutex' scenario described in section 8.2 (which involves waiting for an event and then atomically acquiring a

mutex when the event is finally signalled) could be handled using a
MULTI_EVENT object — in this case the mutex would be simulated using an event
provided by the MULTI_EVENT object so that the 'wait-and-acquire' operation can
be implemented simply by waiting for an event set of size two that comprises the
real event plus the simulated mutex. The attempt at the SYNCH class Wait()
function originally introduced in section 5.8 and discussed further in section 8.2
may be rewritten to use a MULTI_EVENT object in place of separate MUTEX and
EVENT objects as follows:

```
int SYNCH::Wait(void* context) {
  int status;
  int cookies[2] = {0,1};
  do {
    MultiEvent.Wait(cookies,1);
    status = Status(context);
    if (status == SYNCH_WAIT)
      Waiters++;
    MultiEvent.Signal(cookies[0]);
    if (status == SYNCH_WAIT) {
      MultiEvent.Wait(cookies,2,TRUE);
      if (--Runners)
        MultiEvent.Signal(cookies[1]);
      MultiEvent.Signal(cookies[0]);
    }
  } while (status == SYNCH_WAIT);
  return (status == SYNCH_OKAY);
}
```

Here the simulated mutex is acquired and released by making calls to
the MULTI_EVENT object's Wait() and Signal() functions with the
cookies[0] array element being passed as a parameter — the combined
event-wait-and-mutex-acquire operation is achieved with a single call to the
MULTI_EVENT class Wait() function that specifies both the event and the
simulated mutex using the two elements in the cookies array. The next section
covers the MULTI_EVENT class in much more detail.

9.2 The MULTI_EVENT Class

The MULTI_EVENT class embodies the functionality required to safely manipulate
multiple events — as noted in the previous section the two basic capabilities desired
are:

1. to wait for any one out of several possible events to be signalled
2. to wait for a set of events to all be signalled simultaneously

To fulfil these requirements the MULTI_EVENT class has the following specification:

```
class MULTI_EVENT {
public:
  MULTI_EVENT(void);
  ~MULTI_EVENT(void);
  int Wait(int[],int,int = FALSE);
  void Signal(int);
  void Reset(int);
      .
      .
};
```

The third parameter to the MULTI_EVENT class Wait() function (which defaults to FALSE) determines which of the two basic capabilities is being requested — a FALSE value indicates that the function must return as soon as one selected event has been signalled whereas a TRUE value means that the Wait() function must not return until all the selected events are signalled simultaneously. The selected events are specified using the first two parameters to the MULTI_EVENT class Wait() function — the first parameter is an array of integer cookie values 0, 1, 2, ... whilst the second parameter is a count of the number of elements in the array. To call the Wait() function the array of cookies must firstly be set up:

```
int cookies[3] = {1,4,7};
int cookie = MultiEvent.Wait(cookies,3);
```

Here the cookie variable will be set by the return value from the Wait() function to 1, 4 or 7 depending on which event is signalled — if the third parameter to Wait() is set to TRUE so that signalling of all three events must be awaited then the return value will always be zero. As with an ordinary automatic EVENT object, the event or events waited for by the MULTI_EVENT class Wait() function will be set to their non-signalled state whenever the Wait() call completes — however, if the MULTI_EVENT class Wait() function is waiting for all events in some set to be signalled simultaneously this does not preclude other threads from completing Wait() calls for overlapping event sets. The MULTI_EVENT class Signal() and Reset() functions allow the state of individual events within a MULTI_EVENT object to be explicitly updated — both functions take an integer cookie parameter to specify which event to modify and the Signal() function sets the state to signalled whilst the Reset() function resets the state to non-signalled.

As promised in the previous section, the `TICK_TOCK` class provides an example of working with the `MULTI_EVENT` class — the specification for the `TICK_TOCK` class is as follows:

```
class TICK_TOCK {
  class LOOP : public THREAD {
  friend class TICK_TOCK;
  public:
    LOOP(TICK_TOCK*);
    ~LOOP(void);
  protected:
    void* Run(void*);
  private:
    TICK_TOCK* TickTock;
    EVENT Quit;
  };
friend class LOOP;
public:
  TICK_TOCK(void);
  ~TICK_TOCK(void);
private:
  MULTI_EVENT MultiEvent;
  LOOP* Loops[3];
  char* Beat;
};
```

A nested `LOOP` class is used to define the `Run()` function for the secondary threads — this technique is discussed at greater length in the following section. The `TICK_TOCK` class constructor starts up the three threads A, B and C discussed in the previous section:

```
TICK_TOCK::TICK_TOCK(void) {
  MultiEvent.Signal(1);
  char threads[3] = {'C','A','B'};
  for (int i=0; (i<3); i++) {
    Loops[i] = new LOOP(this);
    Loops[i]->Start((void*)threads[i]);
  }
}
```

The constructor also signals event X instead of thread C doing it — the `MultiEvent` object manages the events W, X, Y and Z which are referenced using the cookie values 0, 1, 2 and 3 respectively.

The processing performed by the threads A, B and C is defined by the nested LOOP class Run() function:

```
void* TICK_TOCK::LOOP::Run(void* param) {
  char thread = (char)(long)param;
  int cookies[2];
  do {
    switch (thread) {
    case 'A':
      cookies[0] = 1;
      cookies[1] = 3;
      TickTock->MultiEvent.Wait(cookies,2,TRUE);
      TickTock->Beat = "Tick";
      TickTock->MultiEvent.Signal(2);
      TickTock->MultiEvent.Signal(0);
      break;
    case 'B':
      cookies[0] = 2;
      cookies[1] = 3;
      TickTock->MultiEvent.Wait(cookies,2,TRUE);
      TickTock->Beat = "Tock";
      TickTock->MultiEvent.Signal(1);
      TickTock->MultiEvent.Signal(0);
      break;
    case 'C':
      TickTock->MultiEvent.Signal(3);
      Sleep(100);
      cookies[0] = 0;
      TickTock->MultiEvent.Wait(cookies,1);
      printf("%s\n",TickTock->Beat);
      break;
    }
  } while (!Quit.Test());
  return NULL;
}
```

The TICK_TOCK class destructor brings the three threads to a halt by signalling the Quit events embedded by the LOOP objects, firstly stopping thread C and then threads A and B — however, the destructor must ensure that a thread cannot hang whilst waiting for an unsignalled event and the resultant details are sufficiently untidy to warrant omission.

9.3 Random Event Monitoring

To provide a more comprehensive illustration of applying the MULTI_EVENT class this section and the next discuss an example of 'random event monitoring' — as explained in section 9.1 this technique is in general useful whenever a single thread must handle multiple events that can be signalled in an unpredictable order. Here the random events are generated by a collection of HELLO objects which send greetings messages quite independently of one another — the events are monitored by a GOODBYE object which listens simultaneously to all the HELLO objects:

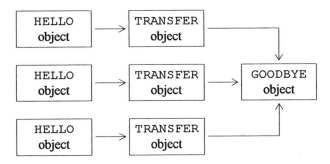

This section covers the GOODBYE class whilst the next section deals with an updated version of the HELLO class first introduced in section 2.4. — section 6.2 describes the operation of the intermediary TRANSFER class in detail. The specification for the GOODBYE class is as follows:

```
class GOODBYE {
  class LOOP : public THREAD {
  friend class GOODBYE;
      ...
  };
  class TIMEOUT : public TIMER_ACTIVITY {
  friend class GOODBYE;
      ...
  };
  friend class LOOP;
  friend class TIMEOUT;
public:
  GOODBYE(TRANSFER_INTERFACE**,int);
  ~GOODBYE(void);
  int Print(void);
private:
  void Reset(void);
  int ThreadCount;
  int Cookies[GOODBYE_MAX_THREADS+1];
  LOOP* Loops[GOODBYE_MAX_THREADS];
  TRANSFER_INTERFACE** Transfers;
  MULTI_EVENT MultiEvent;
  TIMEOUT* Timeout;
  int TimeoutID;
  static TIMER Timer;
  MUTEX Mutex;
};
```

The GOODBYE class uses an external 'master' thread to monitor the random events produced whenever the HELLO objects send their messages — there is also one internal 'slave' thread for each HELLO object which actually receives messages from that object and signals the associated event. The nested LOOP class provides the GOODBYE object's slave threads whilst the nested TIMEOUT class defines a timer activity which causes the GOODBYE class Print() function to time out if no messages are received from any HELLO objects within a certain interval. The maximum number of slave threads and the timeout interval (in 'ticks') are fixed by the following constants:

```
const int GOODBYE_MAX_THREADS = 10;
const int GOODBYE_TIMEOUT = 100;
```

The **friend** keyword is sprinkled liberally about to allow objects from the three classes (GOODBYE, LOOP and TIMEOUT) to freely manipulate one another's private data — this may appear to contradict the object-oriented quest for data encapsulation but in fact the GOODBYE object and its assorted helper objects should be viewed as a single entity with no internal barriers being necessary. The GOODBYE class maintains pointers to the internal LOOP and TIMEOUT objects using the Loops array and the Timeout field — conversely, the nested LOOP and TIMEOUT classes each define a Goodbye field to hold a pointer back to the main object. The full specification for the nested LOOP class is as follows:

```
class LOOP : public THREAD {
friend class GOODBYE;
public:
  LOOP(GOODBYE*,int);
  ~LOOP(void);
protected:
  virtual void* Run(void*);
private:
  GOODBYE* Goodbye;
  EVENT Ready;
  char* Data;
};
```

And the nested TIMEOUT class has the following specification:

```
class TIMEOUT : public TIMER_ACTIVITY {
friend class GOODBYE;
public:
  TIMEOUT(GOODBYE*);
  ~TIMEOUT(void);
  virtual void Trigger(void);
private:
  GOODBYE* Goodbye;
};
```

The GOODBYE class constructor initializes the collection of LOOP and TIMEOUT objects contained by each GOODBYE object — it also sets the corresponding entries in the Cookies array:

```
GOODBYE::GOODBYE(TRANSFER_INTERFACE** transfers,
                int thread_count) {
  int i;
  Transfers = transfers;
  ThreadCount = thread_count;
  for (i=0; (i<ThreadCount); i++) {
    Loops[i] = new LOOP(this,i);
    Cookies[i] = i;
  }
  Timeout = new TIMEOUT(this);
  Cookies[i] = i;
}
```

Furthermore, the constructor stores an array of TRANSFER_INTERFACE* pointers passed in as a parameter — the referenced TRANSFER objects will be used to receive greetings messages from the HELLO objects. The second parameter to the GOODBYE class constructor specifies the number of TRANSFER object pointers in the array — an equal number of LOOP objects are created by the constructor so that there is one slave thread listening to each HELLO object. The TIMEOUT class constructor simply stores the back-pointer to the GOODBYE object:

```
GOODBYE::TIMEOUT::TIMEOUT(GOODBYE* goodbye) {
  Goodbye = goodbye;
}
```

The LOOP class constructor does likewise but it also starts the internal slave thread:

```
GOODBYE::LOOP::LOOP(GOODBYE* goodbye,int id) {
  Goodbye = goodbye;
  Start((void*)id);
}
```

The id parameter passed along by Start() to the LOOP class Run() function identifies the individual slave threads and serves two purposes — firstly, the identifier indexes into the GOODBYE object's array of TRANSFER_INTERFACE* pointers so that the thread knows which HELLO object to listen to and secondly, the identifier acts as a unique 'cookie' to pass to the MULTI_EVENT object embedded within the GOODBYE object and so it ties each slave thread to a particular event.

The LOOP class Run() function loops repeatedly listening for messages from the associated HELLO object:

```
void* GOODBYE::LOOP::Run(void* param) {
  int id = (int)(long)param;
  int length;
  while (Goodbye->Transfers[id]->Receive(&Data,&length))
  {
    Goodbye->MultiEvent.Signal(id);
    Ready.Wait();
    delete [] Data;
  }
  return NULL;
}
```

Each message received is stored in the LOOP object's Data field and then the GOODBYE object is notified by signalling its embedded MULTI_EVENT object — the LOOP object subsequently waits on its Ready event until the GOODBYE object acknowledges that it has processed the data. This is another example of the 'producer-consumer' paradigm discussed in sections 4.3 and 4.4 — here the LOOP object is the producer and the GOODBYE object is the consumer whilst the two events needed to regulate the interaction are provided by the MULTI_EVENT object and the LOOP object's embedded EVENT object. The GOODBYE class destructor breaks all the LOOP class Run() functions out of their **while** loops:

```
GOODBYE::~GOODBYE(void) {
  for (int i=0; (i<ThreadCount); i++) {
    Transfers[i]->Break();
    Loops[i]->Ready.Signal();
    delete Loops[i];
  }
  delete Timeout;
  printf("Goodbye\n");
}
```

For each slave thread the GOODBYE class destructor calls the Break() function of the corresponding TRANSFER object and this causes the TRANSFER class Receive() function to return FALSE thereby terminating the Run() function's loop — the destructor also signals the LOOP object's Ready event in case the slave thread has already received some data and is in the process of making a call to the EVENT class Wait() function. The GOODBYE class destructor may be held up each time it deletes a LOOP object since it must wait whilst the LOOP class destructor ensures that the internal slave thread has terminated:

```
GOODBYE::LOOP::~LOOP(void) {
  Wait();
}
```

However, the TIMEOUT class destructor performs no processing:

```
GOODBYE::TIMEOUT::~TIMEOUT(void) {}
```

Between creation and destruction the GOODBYE object relies on an external thread to repeatedly call the GOODBYE class Print() function and so serve as the master thread which coordinates the activities of the GOODBYE object:

```
int GOODBYE::Print(void) {
  int status = FALSE;
  TimeoutID =
    Timer.Schedule(Timeout,GOODBYE_TIMEOUT,&Mutex);
  int i = MultiEvent.Wait(Cookies,ThreadCount+1);
  if (i < ThreadCount) {
    printf(Loops[i]->Data);
    Loops[i]->Ready.Signal();
    status = TRUE;
  }
  Reset();
  return status;
}
```

The heart of the Print() function is the call to the MULTI_EVENT class Wait() function — this function blocks until one of the slave threads signals an event and then it returns the cookie passed by the slave thread to the MULTI_EVENT class Signal() function. Upon receipt of the signal the master thread assumes its role as consumer of the data produced by the slave thread — the greetings message is printed out and afterwards the slave thread's Ready event is signalled. Actually, this procedure is only followed in the normal course of events and in this case the Print() function returns a TRUE status value to indicate that all went well — however, the operation of the Print() function is complicated by the use of the TIMEOUT object which can cause the Print() function to return a FALSE status value if no message is received from any HELLO object within ten seconds. The timeout period is started at the beginning of the GOODBYE class Print() function with a call to the TIMER class Schedule() function — if the timer activity is triggered then the TIMEOUT class Trigger() function will be invoked:

```
void GOODBYE::TIMEOUT::Trigger(void) {
  Goodbye->MultiEvent.Signal(Goodbye->ThreadCount);
  Goodbye->TimeoutID = -1;
}
```

The Trigger() function signals the embedded MULTI_EVENT object using a cookie value of ThreadCount (and also invalidates the TimeoutID field) — this particular cookie value is not used by any of the slave threads and so the GOODBYE class Print() function can easily determine when a timeout has occurred. Whether a message is received or not the Print() function calls the

GOODBYE class `Reset()` function before returning its status value — the `Reset()` function resets the timeout apparatus to the state it was in before the `Print()` call:

```
void GOODBYE::Reset(void) {
  Mutex.Acquire();
  Timer.Cancel(TimeoutID);
  MultiEvent.Reset(ThreadCount);
  Mutex.Release();
}
```

The `Reset()` function firstly acquires the timer activity mutex in case the timeout is still pending — then either the timer activity is cancelled or the timeout event is reset. The description of the GOODBYE class and its nested classes is now complete — the following section illustrates how to use a GOODBYE object to monitor the random events produced by a collection of HELLO objects.

9.4 The HELLO Class

To provide events for a GOODBYE object to monitor, this section reworks the HELLO class introduced in section 2.4 using some of the techniques discussed in the intervening chapters — firstly, the thread supplied by the THREAD base class is treated as an internal thread of the HELLO object with the object's greeting message being passed via the HELLO class constructor rather than directly to the inherited THREAD class `Start()` function and secondly, the greeting is not printed straight to the screen but instead is transmitted to the GOODBYE object via a transfer object. The revised specification for the HELLO class is as follows:

```
class HELLO : public THREAD {
public:
  HELLO(char*,TRANSFER_INTERFACE*);
  ~HELLO(void);
protected:
  virtual void* Run(void*);
private:
  TRANSFER_INTERFACE* Transfer;
};
```

The HELLO class constructor takes two parameters — the first specifies the greetings message to be sent by the HELLO object whilst the second is a pointer to the TRANSFER object that will convey the message to the GOODBYE object:

```
HELLO::HELLO(char* message,TRANSFER_INTERFACE* transfer)
{
  Transfer = transfer;
  Start(message);
}
```

The TRANSFER_INTERFACE* pointer is stored in the Transfer field whilst the greetings message is passed along to the HELLO class Run() function as a parameter:

```cpp
void* HELLO::Run(void* param) {
  char* message = (char*)param;
  int length = strlen(message)+2;
  char* string;
  for (int i=0; (i<3); i++) {
    string = new char[length];
    sprintf(string,"%s\n",message);
    Transfer->Send(string,length);
    Sleep(100);
  }
  return NULL;
}
```

As in section 2.4 the greetings message is displayed three times at intervals of a tenth of a second — however, the message is now transmitted via the associated TRANSFER object rather than being printed directly. After the three iterations the HELLO object's internal thread exits and is subsequently waited for by the HELLO class destructor:

```cpp
HELLO::~HELLO(void) {
  Wait();
}
```

As in section 2.4 the HELLO class Run() function will be invoked simultaneously by three separate threads each passing in a different message — the main() function is assigned the task of creating the three HELLO objects and it also creates the GOODBYE object and the intermediary TRANSFER objects:

```cpp
int main(int argc, char** argv) {
  int i;
  TRANSFER_INTERFACE* transfers[3];
  for (i=0; (i<3); i++)
    transfers[i] = new TRANSFER;
  {
    HELLO english("Hello",transfers[0]);
    HELLO french("Bonjour",transfers[1]);
    HELLO german("Guten Tag",transfers[2]);
    GOODBYE goodbye(transfers,3);
    while (goodbye.Print());
  }
  for (i=0; (i<3); i++)
    delete transfers[i];
  return 0;
}
```

Once created by the primary thread the HELLO and GOODBYE objects start their secondary threads internally — the assorted greetings are then sent by the HELLO threads through the TRANSFER objects to the GOODBYE object which prints them out one by one as the primary thread repeatedly invokes the GOODBYE class Print() function. After exiting the **while** loop the primary thread is held up at the end of the enclosing block whilst it waits for the HELLO and GOODBYE objects to be destroyed — the HELLO and GOODBYE class destructors both generate calls to the THREAD class Wait() function to ensure that the various internal threads have terminated before the corresponding objects are destroyed. As previously explained the exact ordering of thread execution is unpredictable but the following output from the program is typical:

```
Hello
Bonjour
Guten Tag
Hello
Bonjour
Guten Tag
Hello
Bonjour
Guten Tag
Goodbye
```

Finally, note that the TRANSFER objects could easily be replaced with any other objects which support the interface defined by the TRANSFER_INTERFACE class. For example, the CHANNEL class described in section 10.2 allows data to be transferred across a network connection and so if CHANNEL objects were wrapped with suitable transfer objects then it would be possible to create each of the HELLO and GOODBYE objects on a totally different machine — essentially the same technique is adopted in the following chapter to build a distributed database application.

9.5 UNIX Implementation

Under UNIX the implementation of the MULTI_EVENT class bears a close resemblance to the implementation of the SYNCH class described in section 5.7 — each MULTI_EVENT object embeds both a pthread_cond_t structure plus an associated pthread_mutex_t structure to provide the necessary thread synchronization and the MULTI_EVENT class functions are modelled on those of the SYNCH class. Indeed the major difference between the two classes is that the MULTI_EVENT class defines an Active array to hold the current states of all the events managed internally by the MULTI_EVENT object. The MULTI_EVENT class defines the following associated constants:

```
const int MULTI_EVENT_MAX_EVENTS = 100;
const int MULTI_EVENT_WAIT = 0;
const int MULTI_EVENT_OKAY = 1;
```

The full specification for the MULTI_EVENT class is as follows:

```
class MULTI_EVENT {
public:
  MULTI_EVENT(void);
  ~MULTI_EVENT(void);
  int Wait(int[],int,int = FALSE);
  void Signal(int);
  void Reset(int);
private:
  int Status(int[],int,int);
  pthread_cond_t Event;
  pthread_mutex_t Mutex;
  int Active[MULTI_EVENT_MAX_EVENTS];
};
```

The MULTI_EVENT class constructor initializes the synchronization primitives supplied by the operating system and also sets all the elements in the Active array to FALSE so that the events are all initially non-signalled:

```
MULTI_EVENT::MULTI_EVENT(void) {
  pthread_cond_init(&Event, (pthread_condattr_t*)NULL);
  pthread_mutex_init(&Mutex, (pthread_mutexattr_t*)NULL);
  for (int i=0; (i<MULTI_EVENT_MAX_EVENTS); i++)
    Active[i] = FALSE;
}
```

The MULTI_EVENT class destructor, on the other hand, simply releases the condition variable and associated mutex back to the operating system:

```
MULTI_EVENT::~MULTI_EVENT(void) {
  pthread_cond_destroy(&Event);
  pthread_mutex_destroy(&Mutex);
}
```

The MULTI_EVENT class Wait() function is modelled on the SYNCH class Wait() function from section 5.7:

```
int MULTI_EVENT::Wait(int cookies[],int count,
                               int wait_all) {
  pthread_mutex_lock(&Mutex);
  int status = Status(cookies,count,wait_all);
  while (status == MULTI_EVENT_WAIT) {
    pthread_cond_wait(&Event,&Mutex);
    status = Status(cookies,count,wait_all);
  }
  pthread_mutex_unlock(&Mutex);
  return (status-MULTI_EVENT_OKAY);
}
```

The Wait() function loops repeatedly until the MULTI_EVENT class Status() function stops returning MULTI_EVENT_WAIT and instead indicates that one or all of the events waited upon have been signalled. As with the SYNCH class Wait() function the MULTI_EVENT object's embedded mutex is initially acquired before the loop and is eventually released whenever the loop terminates — with each iteration of the loop the pthread_cond_wait() function temporarily releases the mutex whilst waiting for the embedded event to be signalled but it reacquires the mutex just before returning. When it is waiting for all the events in an event set to be signalled the MULTI_EVENT class Wait() function simply returns zero upon completion — however, if one of several possible events is being awaited then the Wait() function uses the status information provided by the Status() function to return the cookie corresponding to the event which was signalled. The MULTI_EVENT class Status() function checks on the values stored in the Active array to determine the status of a chosen set of events — the Status() function accepts exactly the same three parameters as the Wait() function so that the chosen events are specified by the first two parameters and the third parameter indicates the mode of operation:

```
int MULTI_EVENT::Status(int cookies[],int count,
                              int wait_all) {
  int i;
  int status = (wait_all ?
          MULTI_EVENT_OKAY : MULTI_EVENT_WAIT);
  for (i=0; (i<count); i++)
    if (wait_all) {
      if (!Active[cookies[i]]) {
        status = MULTI_EVENT_WAIT;
        break;
      }
    }
    else if (Active[cookies[i]]) {
      status = (MULTI_EVENT_OKAY+cookies[i]);
      Active[cookies[i]] = FALSE;
      break;
    }
  if (wait_all && (status==MULTI_EVENT_OKAY))
    for (i=0; (i<count); i++)
      Active[cookies[i]] = FALSE;
  return status;
}
```

If the wait_all parameter is TRUE then the Status() function returns MULTI_EVENT_WAIT unless all selected elements in the Active array are TRUE — in that case the function returns MULTI_EVENT_OKAY and sets all the selected array elements to FALSE. Conversely, if the wait_all parameter is FALSE then the `Status()` function returns `MULTI_EVENT_WAIT` only if all selected elements in the `Active` array are `FALSE` — as soon as one selected array element is found that is `TRUE` it is set to `FALSE` and the function returns `MULTI_EVENT_OKAY` plus the index of the element in the array. The `MULTI_EVENT` class `Signal()` function allows elements in the `Active` array to be set to `TRUE` under the protection of the embedded mutex:

```
void MULTI_EVENT::Signal(int cookie) {
  pthread_mutex_lock(&Mutex);
  Active[cookie] = TRUE;
  pthread_cond_broadcast(&Event);
  pthread_mutex_unlock(&Mutex);
}
```

The `Signal()` function also calls `pthread_cond_broadcast()` in case there are any threads waiting in `Wait()` for this particular array element to be set to `TRUE`. The `MULTI_EVENT` class `Reset()` function similarly sets a selected element of the `Active` array to `FALSE` but it makes no call to `pthread_cond_broadcast()` since this is unnecessary:

```
void MULTI_EVENT::Reset(int cookie) {
  pthread_mutex_lock(&Mutex);
  Active[cookie] = FALSE;
  pthread_mutex_unlock(&Mutex);
}
```

The next section carries the similarity between the `SYNCH` and `MULTI_EVENT` classes apparent in this section a stage further — another version of the `MULTI_EVENT` class is derived from the `SYNCH` base class to provide an implementation of the `MULTI_EVENT` class which is independent of the underlying operating system.

9.6 Generic Implementation

This section provides a generic implementation of the `MULTI_EVENT` class by deriving the `MULTI_EVENT` class from the `SYNCH` base class — the context parameters supplied by the `SYNCH` class are used to pass around information in a `MULTI_EVENT_CONTEXT` structure:

```
struct MULTI_EVENT_CONTEXT {
  int* Cookies;
  int Count;
  int WaitAll;
  int Status;
};
```

The full specification for this implementation of the MULTI_EVENT class is as follows:

```
const int MULTI_EVENT_MAX_EVENTS = 100;

class MULTI_EVENT : public SYNCH {
public:
  MULTI_EVENT(void);
  ~MULTI_EVENT(void);
  int Wait(int[],int,int = FALSE);
  void Signal(int);
  void Reset(int);
protected:
  virtual int Status(void*);
  virtual int Update(void*);
private:
  int Active[MULTI_EVENT_MAX_EVENTS];
};
```

The MULTI_EVENT class constructor simply sets the elements in the Active array to FALSE to mark all the events as initially non-signalled whilst the MULTI_EVENT class destructor performs no processing:

```
MULTI_EVENT::MULTI_EVENT(void) {
  for (int i=0; (i<MULTI_EVENT_MAX_EVENTS); i++)
    Active[i] = FALSE;
}

MULTI_EVENT::~MULTI_EVENT(void) {}
```

The MULTI_EVENT class Wait() function just packages up its parameters in a MULTI_EVENT_CONTEXT structure and passes it along to the base class Wait() function — after the call to the base class function the Status field of the MULTI_EVENT_CONTEXT structure holds the status value to return from the MULTI_EVENT class Wait() function:

```
int MULTI_EVENT::Wait(int cookies[],int count,
                             int wait_all) {
  MULTI_EVENT_CONTEXT context;
  context.Cookies = cookies;
  context.Count = count;
  context.WaitAll = wait_all;
  SYNCH::Wait(&context);
  return (context.Status);
}
```

The SYNCH class Wait() function calls the virtual Status() function overridden by the MULTI_EVENT class:

```
int MULTI_EVENT::Status(void* param) {
  MULTI_EVENT_CONTEXT* context =
                      (MULTI_EVENT_CONTEXT*)param;
  int* cookies = context->Cookies;
  int count = context->Count;
  int wait_all = context->WaitAll;
  int status = (wait_all ? SYNCH_OKAY : SYNCH_WAIT);
  int i;
  context->Status = 0;
  for (i=0; (i<count); i++)
    if (wait_all) {
      if (!Active[cookies[i]]) {
        status = SYNCH_WAIT;
        break;
      }
    }
    else if (Active[cookies[i]]) {
      Active[cookies[i]] = FALSE;
      context->Status = cookies[i];
      status = SYNCH_OKAY;
      break;
    }
  if (wait_all && (status==SYNCH_OKAY))
    for (i=0; (i<count); i++)
      Active[cookies[i]] = FALSE;
  return status;
}
```

The MULTI_EVENT class Status() function unpacks the information contained in the MULTI_EVENT_CONTEXT structure and then follows pretty much the same logic as in the previous section to examine the Active array and determine a status result — note that the status value is split into two parts with the return value from the Status() function being consumed by the SYNCH class Wait() function and the Status field of the MULTI_EVENT_CONTEXT structure supplying the cookie value to be returned by the MULTI_EVENT class Wait() function. The MULTI_EVENT class Signal() and Reset() functions are practically identical — the Signal() function has the following definition:

```
void MULTI_EVENT::Signal(int cookie) {
  MULTI_EVENT_CONTEXT context;
  context.Cookies = &cookie;
  context.Status = TRUE;
  Broadcast(&context);
}
```

And the `Reset()` function is defined as follows:

```
void MULTI_EVENT::Reset(int cookie) {
  MULTI_EVENT_CONTEXT context;
  context.Cookies = &cookie;
  context.Status = FALSE;
  Broadcast(&context);
}
```

The only difference between the two functions is that `Signal()` sets the `Status` field of the context parameter to `TRUE` whereas the `Reset()` function sets the field to `FALSE`. Both functions invoke the `SYNCH` class `Broadcast()` function which generates calls to the virtual function `Update()` overridden by the `MULTI_EVENT` class:

```
int MULTI_EVENT::Update(void* param) {
  MULTI_EVENT_CONTEXT* context =
                      (MULTI_EVENT_CONTEXT*)param;
  int cookie = context->Cookies[0];
  return (Active[cookie] = context->Status);
}
```

The `Update()` function sets the chosen element of the `Active` array to either `TRUE` or `FALSE` according to whether `Signal()` or `Reset()` has been called — the `Update()` function returns a `TRUE` value to indicate that a signal should be broadcast to any threads waiting in `Wait()` only if the `Active` array element is set to `TRUE`.

9.7 Windows Implementation

The Windows operating system provides direct support for multiple events through its `WaitForMultipleObjects()` function — this considerably simplifies the implementation of the `MULTI_EVENT` class under Windows. The specification for the `MULTI_EVENT` class is as follows:

```
const int MULTI_EVENT_MAX_EVENTS = 100;

class MULTI_EVENT {
public:
  MULTI_EVENT(void);
  ~MULTI_EVENT(void);
  int Wait(int[],int,int = FALSE);
  void Signal(int);
  void Reset(int);
private:
  HANDLE Handles[MULTI_EVENT_MAX_EVENTS];
};
```

Each MULTI_EVENT object holds an array of handles to Windows event objects —
the MULTI_EVENT class constructor is responsible for initially creating all these
events:

```
MULTI_EVENT::MULTI_EVENT(void) {
  for (int i=0; (i<MULTI_EVENT_MAX_EVENTS); i++)
    Handles[i] = CreateEvent(NULL,FALSE,FALSE,NULL);
}
```

Similarly, the MULTI_EVENT class destructor releases all the event objects back to
the operating system:

```
MULTI_EVENT::~MULTI_EVENT(void) {
  for (int i=0; (i<MULTI_EVENT_MAX_EVENTS); i++)
    CloseHandle(Handles[i]);
}
```

The MULTI_EVENT class Wait() function simply translates its parameter array
of cookies into an array of event handles and then calls the Windows function
WaitForMultipleObjects() to do all the hard work:

```
int MULTI_EVENT::Wait(int cookies[],int count,
                      int wait_all) {
  HANDLE handles[MULTI_EVENT_MAX_EVENTS];
  for (int i=0; (i<count); i++)
    handles[i] = Handles[cookies[i]];
  int status = WaitForMultipleObjects(count,handles,
                            wait_all,INFINITE);
  return (wait_all ? 0 : cookies[status-WAIT_OBJECT_0]);
}
```

Whenever one out of several events is being awaited the status result from the
Windows function must be translated back into the appropriate cookie value —
conversely, after waiting for an entire event set to be signalled the Wait()
function always returns zero. The MULTI_EVENT class Signal() function calls
the Windows SetEvent() function passing in the handle of the selected event:

```
void MULTI_EVENT::Signal(int cookie) {
  SetEvent(Handles[cookie]);
}
```

The MULTI_EVENT class Reset() function similarly calls the Windows
function ResetEvent() to reset the chosen event:

```
void MULTI_EVENT::Reset(int cookie) {
  ResetEvent(Handles[cookie]);
}
```

9.8 Summary

The problem with managing multiple events is that it is generally impossible to predict the exact order in which the various events will be signalled — the two basic modes of operation involve either waiting for one out of several possible events to be signalled or alternatively waiting for all events in a set to become signalled simultaneously. In the first case the waiting thread does not know which of the events to expect next and so must monitor them all — this activity is termed 'random event monitoring' and a common example occurs during input/output processing when a number of concurrent read or write operations are scheduled and a collection of events are used to signal completion of the various requests. In the second case (where entire sets of events are waited for) the complications arise whenever several threads are waiting for some of the same events to be signalled so that the event sets overlap — if some events in a set are signalled whilst others are not then a thread cannot just accept the pending signals immediately lest it holds up another thread which is waiting for those events to be signalled as part of another overlapping event set. The MULTI_EVENT class is specifically designed to support the two basic modes of handling multiple events — each MULTI_EVENT object maintains a collection of events internally and these are referenced by external code using unique integer cookie values 0, 1, 2, ... and so on. Implementations for UNIX and Windows operating systems have been described along with a generic version that builds on the services of the SYNCH class to provide an implementation that is independent of the underlying operating system — in particular, Windows provides direct support for multiple events through the WaitForMultipleObjects() function and the Windows implementation of the MULTI_EVENT class functions are essentially wrappers for operating system functions. The MULTI_EVENT class Wait() function allows a thread to wait for one event out of several selected events to be signalled or alternatively the Wait() function can be instructed to wait for an entire set of selected events to become signalled — in both cases the events are specified using an array of cookie values and in the first case the cookie corresponding to the signalled event is returned from the Wait() function. As with ordinary automatic EVENT objects the MULTI_EVENT class Wait() function resets the event or events it has waited for to their non-signalled state before returning — the state of individual events within a MULTI_EVENT object may be explicitly updated to the signalled or non-signalled state simply by passing the appropriate cookie value to the MULTI_EVENT class functions Signal() and Reset(). To illustrate how to apply the functionality provided by the MULTI_EVENT class the chapter updated the HELLO class to send a series of greetings messages to a GOODBYE object — the GOODBYE class monitors the arrival of the messages using an embedded MULTI_EVENT object and also runs a number of internal threads that each listen to one HELLO object and signal the corresponding event as required. The GOODBYE class also incorporates an internal timer that signals yet another event if there is no input from the HELLO objects within a certain period. Finally, the TICK_TOCK class was introduced to illustrate the handling of overlapping event sets — although somewhat contrived the example does at least highlight some of the complications that can occur with multiple events.

10. Distributed Computing

It is traditional to end a book such as this with an extensive example of the subject in hand — however, it is all too easy to throw caution to the wind and create a monster application which is far more complex than anything that has appeared in earlier chapters. The aim of this chapter therefore is to develop an extended example of multi-threaded programming in C++ which is reasonably simple, which demonstrates some of the techniques previously introduced in a fairly realistic setting and finally, which could be enhanced to create a more substantial application if so desired. The example actually chosen is a 'distributed database' application which comprises a database 'server' running on one computer that can be queried for information by 'client' programs running on other machines distributed throughout a network. The main topics covered in the chapter include:

— network communications
— packets and streams
— the CHANNEL class
— the STREAM class
— relational databases
— the QUERY class
— the DATABASE class

The database server could certainly be written as a single-threaded application but assigning various tasks (such as talking to clients or working with the database) to different threads simplifies the design of the individual components somewhat — this fact will become more and more important as the complexity of the application grows.

10.1 Network Communications

In the good old days computers operated in isolation with a lone mainframe machine typically housed in an air-conditioned room and connected to a number of dumb terminals by dedicated serial lines of several metres length. The situation gradually improved with the introduction of computer networks that allowed several computers owned by the same institution to talk to one another — nonetheless, the advent of the personal computer unleashed large numbers of unconnected microprocessors into the world. More recently, however, and especially since the explosive growth of the Internet, practically everything is connected to everything else — in fact many companies are now throwing up isolationary 'fire-walls' and running their own intranets just so they can get a little

peace and quiet away from the world wide web of computer nasties such as viruses
and spam. Anyway, network communications is currently a vital element in many
computer applications and so will serve in this chapter as a backdrop for
an extended example of multi-threaded programming — later sections in the
chapter develop a 'distributed database' application that utilizes many of the
multi-threading techniques discussed throughout the book.

There are a wide range of 'network communications protocols' that each specify
exactly how one computer can talk to another — however, a very common example
which is supported by both Windows and UNIX systems is the TCP/IP suite
of communications protocols. The TCP/IP suite (named after its constituent
Internet (IP) and Transmission Control (TCP) protocols) was first introduced as
part of the fledgling Internet and it deals with 'hosts', 'ports' and 'sockets' —
a 'host' is just a fancy name for a computer, a 'port' is an individual connection
point on a host so that each host can support many ports, and finally a 'socket' is a
programmatic device that can be associated with a port to form one end of a
connection. The following figure illustrates how TCP/IP allows two computers to
set up a connection between themselves across which they are able to communicate:

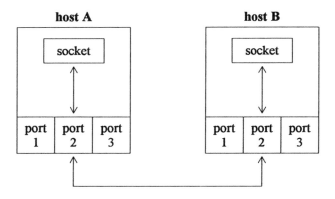

The socket on host A is bound to port 2 on this machine and similarly the socket at
the other end of the connection is bound to port 2 on host B — for a TCP
connection the four quantities comprising the pair of host names and the pair of
port numbers uniquely identify the connection and, in particular, there is no
requirement that the port numbers at either end of the connection be the same.
The sockets are created with the socket() function and then the connection is
established by calling the functions bind(), listen() and accept() on one
side and calling the function connect() on the other side — once the machines
have a connection they can communicate by sending data with the send()
function and receiving data with the recv() function. The asymmetric procedure
for establishing a connection stems from the fact that one machine participating in

the connection is frequently a 'server' whilst the other is a 'client' — the server accepts connections from clients and performs certain processing when requested to do so by them. The DATABASE class described in section 10.7 will act as a server retrieving selected information from a central database — the QUERY class described in section 10.6 supports clients wishing to query the server for information. Since server and clients can each run on a separate machine the whole application is 'distributed' across the network — the result is thus a distributed database application.

10.2 The CHANNEL Class

The CHANNEL class is designed to encapsulate the functionality of a TCP connection — for definiteness an implementation of the CHANNEL class under Windows is presented here although the implementation under the various flavours of UNIX is similar if not without its pitfalls. The specification for the CHANNEL class is as follows:

```
class CHANNEL {
public:
  CHANNEL(void);
  ~CHANNEL(void);
  void Connect(const char*,int);
  void Disconnect(void);
  int Send(char*,int);
  int Receive(char*,int);
private:
  SOCKET GetSocket(void);
  SOCKET Socket;
  MUTEX Mutex;
};
```

Under Windows the CHANNEL class constructor must call the Windows Sockets Application function WSAStartup() to initialize the sockets library:

```
CHANNEL::CHANNEL(void) {
  WSADATA info;
  WSAStartup(0x0202,&info);
}
```

The constant 0x0202 specifies version 2.2 of the library and should be changed as appropriate. The CHANNEL class destructor similarly calls the WSACleanup() function:

```
CHANNEL::~CHANNEL(void) {
  WSACleanup();
}
```

Neither the WSAStartup() function nor the WSACleanup() function is available on a UNIX system and equivalent calls are typically unnecessary. The CHANNEL class Connect() function is responsible for establishing a TCP connection — the function will not return until the connection is made:

```cpp
void CHANNEL::Connect(const char* server,int port) {
  SOCKET socket = ::socket(AF_INET,SOCK_STREAM,0);
  int length = sizeof(sockaddr_in);
  sockaddr_in address;
  address.sin_family = AF_INET;
  address.sin_port = htons((WORD)port);
  if (server == NULL) {
    address.sin_addr.s_addr = INADDR_ANY;
    bind(socket,(sockaddr*)&address,length);
    listen(socket,1);
    Socket = accept(socket,NULL,NULL);
    closesocket(socket);
    socket = ::socket(AF_INET,SOCK_STREAM,0);
    address.sin_port = 0;
    bind(socket,(sockaddr*)&address,length);
    getsockname(socket,(sockaddr*)&address,&length);
    listen(socket,1);
    Send((char*)&(address.sin_port),
            sizeof(unsigned short));
    SOCKET s = Socket;
    Socket = accept(socket,NULL,NULL);
    closesocket(socket);
    closesocket(s);
  }
  else {
    hostent* host = gethostbyname(server);
    memcpy(&(address.sin_addr),
             host->h_addr,sizeof(in_addr));
    while (connect(socket,(sockaddr*)&address,length)
                 == SOCKET_ERROR) {
      closesocket(socket);
      socket = ::socket(AF_INET,SOCK_STREAM,0);
      THREAD::Sleep(1000);
    }
    Socket = socket;
    socket = ::socket(AF_INET,SOCK_STREAM,0);
    Receive((char*)&(address.sin_port),
            sizeof(unsigned short));
    connect(socket,(sockaddr*)&address,length);
    closesocket(Socket);
    Socket = socket;
  }
}
```

On the server the first parameter to the Connect() function is NULL and the socket is bound to the port specified by the second parameter — the server then calls the `accept()` function to wait for a client to make a connection at the 'well-known' port. Meanwhile on the client the parameters to the `Connect()` function specify the host name of the server and the port number on the server to which the client should initially connect — these values are passed as part of the `address` structure to `connect()` and this function is called repeatedly until the server accepts the connection request. The server then makes a new socket and binds it to an arbitrary port — the `getsockname()` function is called to obtain the port number assigned by the operating system and this is passed to the client via the original connection using the CHANNEL class `Send()` and `Receive()` functions. Now the server calls `accept()` again and the client calls `connect()` again but this time the new port on the server is involved — once the new connection is made, the old one is closed and the CHANNEL class `Connect()` function returns on both sides. All these contortions are simply to allow the next CHANNEL object created on the server to re-use the well-known port number — if the server and client were simply to continue communicating over the first connection that they establish then that particular port would no longer be available on the server. As an example of using the CHANNEL class, the following `Connect()` calls can be issued on a server called `arthur` and a client called `guinevere`:

server   **client**

.   .

```
channel.Connect((char*)NULL,5000);        .
                           channel.Connect("arthur",5000);
```

.   .

The CHANNEL class `Disconnect()` function must not be called until the `Connect()` function has returned after establishing the connection and setting the `Socket` field — with a little extra effort the `Disconnect()` function could be made to interrupt an incomplete `Connect()` call but the easy route is chosen here. Under Windows the `Disconnect()` function calls the `closesocket()` function to terminate the connection and interrupt any CHANNEL class `Send()` or `Receive()` calls currently in progress:

```
void CHANNEL::Disconnect(void) {
  Mutex.Acquire();
  closesocket(Socket);
  Socket = INVALID_SOCKET;
  Mutex.Release();
}
```

The `Disconnect()` function is mutex protected since it must set the `Socket` field to `INVALID_SOCKET` to indicate that it is no longer valid.

The CHANNEL class GetSocket() function allows other threads calling Send() or Receive() to safely retrieve the socket handle:

```
SOCKET CHANNEL::GetSocket(void) {
  Mutex.Acquire();
  SOCKET socket = Socket;
  Mutex.Release();
  return socket;
}
```

The CHANNEL class Send() function attempts to send the requested number of characters from a buffer across the network connection — the function returns the actual number of characters sent or returns -1 if an error occurs:

```
int CHANNEL::Send(char* data,int length) {
  int count = 0;
  int status;
  while (count < length) {
    status =
      send(GetSocket(),data+count,length-count,0);
    if (status > 0)
      count += status;
    else {
      count = -1;
      break;
    }
  }
  return count;
}
```

The CHANNEL class Receive() function similarly attempts to fill a buffer with the requested number of characters received from the network connection and it returns the number of characters actually received or returns -1 if an error occurs:

```
int CHANNEL::Receive(char* data,int length) {
  int count = 0;
  int status;
  while (count < length) {
    status =
      recv(GetSocket(),data+count,length-count,0);
    if (status > 0)
      count += status;
    else {
      count = -1;
      break;
    }
  }
  return count;
}
```

The implementation of the CHANNEL class is satisfactory for demonstration purposes but it is not terribly robust. For example, there is a small probability that the CHANNEL class Send() and Receive() functions will malfunction — this could happen under the following set of circumstances:

1. the CHANNEL class GetSocket() function returns a valid socket handle to a thread executing the Send() or Receive() function

2. the CHANNEL class Disconnect() function invalidates the Socket field when the connection is closed

3. the socket handle is reassigned by the operating system to a new socket whenever another thread in the process calls socket() and then this new socket is used to open another connection

4. the send() function within Send() or the recv() function within Receive() uses the handle supplied by GetSocket() in step 1 to communicate via the wrong socket

The current implementation relies on the fact that steps 2 and 3 would have to occur between the evaluation of a function parameter (step 1) and the corresponding function invocation (step 4) whereas these activities are likely to follow one another in quick succession. Furthermore, the problem does not actually apply to the DATABASE or QUERY classes because the only thread which calls Send() and Receive() for a particular CHANNEL object is the same one that invokes its Disconnect() function. Nonetheless, thinking such as this is valuable in ensuring the robustness of a multi-threaded program.

Anyway, ignoring all such considerations, the following code snippet illustrates the typical operation of a CHANNEL object:

```
CHANNEL channel;
channel.Connect("arthur",5000);
    ...
channel.Send(buffer,length);
    ...
channel.Receive(buffer,length);
    ...
channel.Disconnect();
```

The STREAM class described in section 10.4 uses an embedded CHANNEL object to permit streams of bytes to be transmitted between different machines — the next section introduces the STREAM_INTERFACE class from which the STREAM class is derived.

10.3 Packets and Streams

The TRANSFER_INTERFACE class defined in section 6.2 enables packets of data to be transferred from object to object in a standardized manner — this section considers an alternative communication protocol based on the

STREAM_INTERFACE class. The packet transfer mechanism is typically used by the lower layers of a network communications system — the individual packets can be verified upon receipt to discover whether they have been corrupted during transmission. However, it is often more convenient for a data source to communicate with a data sink using a continuous stream of bytes — the higher layers in the network communications system typically provide this service by fragmenting the stream into packets on the sender machine, transmitting the packets using the lower level transport support and then recombining the packets back into a stream at the receiver. The overall scheme is illustrated in the following figure:

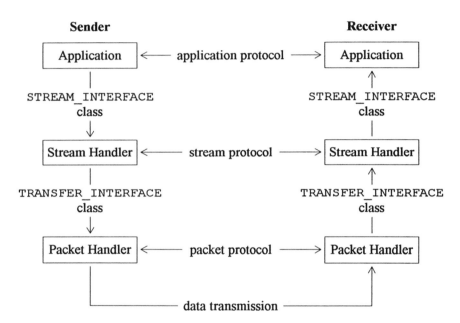

The application layer logically communicates using its application protocol whilst the stream and packet handlers within the communications system respectively use stream and packet protocols — however, the actual flow of data is through the stream and packet interfaces and across the data transmission path. As defined in section 6.2 the TRANSFER_INTERFACE class has the following specification:

```
class TRANSFER_INTERFACE {
public:
  virtual int Send(char*,int) = 0;
  virtual int Receive(char**,int*) = 0;
  virtual void Break(void) = 0;
};
```

The specification for the STREAM_INTERFACE class is similar:

```
class STREAM_INTERFACE {
public:
  virtual int Write(char*,int) = 0;
  virtual int Read(char*,int) = 0;
  virtual void Close(void) = 0;
};
```

Principally to illustrate an alternative approach, the STREAM_INTERFACE class Write() and Read() functions handle their data buffer parameter in a somewhat different manner to the TRANSFER_INTERFACE class Send() and Receive() functions. The buffer passed to the Send() function is allocated by the caller and released by the callee — similarly, the Receive() function creates its buffer internally and this is deleted by the calling code after the data has been processed. However, for both the Write() and Read() functions the data buffer is provided by external code and remains the responsibility of the caller throughout. The second parameter passed to Write() and Read() specifies the size of the write or read request (and so represents the minimum possible length of the buffer) whereas the return value from these functions indicates the number of bytes actually written or read — if an error occurs during a Write() or Read() call then the return value is -1. The following example illustrates transmission of a string with the terminating null character specifically omitted:

```
                .                              .
stream.Write("Hello",5);       char buffer[6];
                .              int length
                .                = stream.Read(buffer,5);
                .              if (length > 0) {
                .                buffer[length] = 0;
                .                printf("%s",buffer);
                .              }
                .                              .
```

The STREAM_INTERFACE class Close() function works in a similar way to the TRANSFER_INTERFACE class Break() function — whenever Close() is invoked any Write() or Read() calls that are currently in progress terminate abruptly and subsequent calls to these functions fail without blocking. For a transfer object the transfer of packets is initially enabled and for a stream object the stream is initially connected — the Break() function disables packet transfer and the Close() function disconnects the stream connection.

The following figure shows the state transition diagrams for transfer and stream objects:

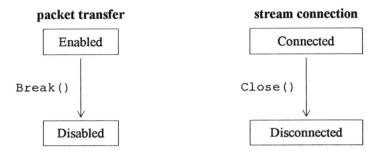

This arrangement is probably the simplest practical way of managing these communication mechanisms. However, it is sometimes convenient to be able to re-enable a packet transfer or reconnect a stream — the following figure shows the state transition diagrams for such 'reusable' transfer and stream objects:

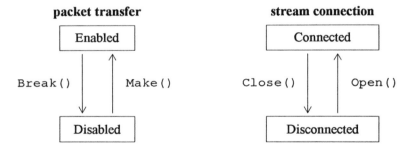

The Make() function and the Open() function respectively belong to the REUSABLE_TRANSFER_INTERFACE and REUSABLE_STREAM_INTERFACE classes — this pair of classes derive from the basic TRANSFER_INTERFACE and STREAM_INTERFACE classes as follows:

```cpp
class REUSABLE_TRANSFER_INTERFACE
  : public TRANSFER_INTERFACE {
public:
  virtual void Make(void) = 0;
  virtual int Enabled(void) = 0;
};

class REUSABLE_STREAM_INTERFACE
  : public STREAM_INTERFACE {
public:
  virtual void Open(void) = 0;
  virtual int Connected(void) = 0;
};
```

The `Make()` and `Open()` functions result in a transition to the active state (`Enabled` or `Connected`) — if the packet transfer is already enabled the `Make()` function has no effect and similarly if the stream is already connected then `Open()` does nothing. In fact the `Make()` and `Open()` functions are exact counterparts of the `Break()` and `Close()` functions except in one important respect — there is a possibility that the `Make()` and `Open()` functions will fail leaving the communications system in the `Disabled` or `Disconnected` state. Consequently, the `REUSABLE_TRANSFER_INTERFACE` class provides the `Enabled()` function to assist external code in tracking the current state of the transfer object and the `REUSABLE_STREAM_INTERFACE` class similarly supplies the `Connected()` function to return the current stream connection status. A reusable transfer object can initially be enabled or disabled — likewise a stream object can initially be connected or disconnected. If a reusable object is documented as initializing into the inactive state then a call to `Make()` or `Open()` will be necessary before the object can be used — conversely, if a reusable object is to be treated as if it were non-reusable then its documentation must state that it initializes into the active state. The interfaces for reusable transfer and stream objects can be quite complicated to implement reliably and so only the basic `TRANSFER_INTERFACE` and `STREAM_INTERFACE` classes are considered in this book — in particular, the following section discusses the implementation of the `STREAM` class which supports the basic stream interface.

10.4 The `STREAM` Class

With the `CHANNEL` class already defined the implementation of the `STREAM` class is very straightforward — the `STREAM` class functions are simply wrappers for the `CHANNEL` class equivalents and the `STREAM` class just serves to implement the stream interface specified by the `STREAM_INTERFACE` class. A similar approach could be adopted to wrap the `CHANNEL` class using a transfer class derived from the `TRANSFER_INTERFACE` class — as mentioned in sections 6.3 and 9.4 this derived class would be a good substitute for the `TRANSFER` class of section 6.2 whenever network communications are required. The full specification for the `STREAM` class is as follows:

```
class STREAM : public STREAM_INTERFACE {
public:
   STREAM(const char*,int);
   ~STREAM(void);
   virtual int Write(char*,int);
   virtual int Read(char*,int);
   virtual void Close(void);
private:
   CHANNEL Channel;
};
```

The STREAM class constructor calls the Connect() function of the embedded CHANNEL object in order to place the STREAM object initially in its active state — the construction process may take some time if the connection cannot be made immediately.

```
STREAM::STREAM(const char* host,int port) {
  Channel.Connect(host,port);
}
```

The STREAM class destructor ends the connection if it has not already been broken:

```
STREAM::~STREAM(void) {
  Close();
}
```

The STREAM class Write() function just delegates to the CHANNEL class Send() function:

```
int STREAM::Write(char* data,int length) {
  return Channel.Send(data,length);
}
```

Similarly the STREAM class Read() function relies on the services of the CHANNEL class Receive() function:

```
int STREAM::Read(char* data,int length) {
  return Channel.Receive(data,length);
}
```

Finally, the STREAM class Close() function calls the CHANNEL class function Disconnect() to close the connection:

```
void STREAM::Close(void) {
  Channel.Disconnect();
}
```

The STREAM class will be used in sections 10.6 and 10.7 to connect QUERY objects on the various client machines to the DATABASE object acting as the server for the distributed database.

10.5 Database Queries

A database forms a repository for information relating to a collection of items — typical examples include:

— the customer account details held by a bank or other business

— the latest stocks and shares prices

— the names and numbers in a telephone directory

Indeed many computer applications today are concerned with processing this sort of information and 'database management systems' are definitely in fashion — in particular, a certain type of database known as a 'relational database' is especially popular thus making RDBMS (Relational DataBase Management System) a common acronym in the computer world. A relational database actually just comprises a set of cross-referenced tables — each table contains a series of rows that individually describe a particular database entry with the various columns each containing a different variety of information about those entries. For example, a simple relational database might have only a single table with two columns:

name	number
arthur	123
guinevere	123
lancelot	456
merlin	789

The 'name' column contains the names of different people and the 'number' column provides the corresponding telephone numbers — in fact, this is the database that will be implemented by the DATABASE class in section 10.7. An essential feature of a relational database is that in each table one or more columns provide a 'key' that uniquely identifies each row — in the above example the 'name' column serves this purpose since all the names are different. The remaining columns in the table are not constrained in this way and may contain duplicated entries — for example, arthur and guinevere share the same telephone number. One particular use for the additional columns is to establish cross-references between tables — this feature is not present in the simple database application described in this chapter but it could easily be included if desired. To provide an example of cross-referencing, the database table above may be extended as follows:

name	number	salary
arthur	123	immense
guinevere	123	good
lancelot	456	pitiful
merlin	789	good

The values in the final column reference entries in another table that supplies more information:

salary	annual income
immense	1000 sacks of gold
good	100 bags of silver
basic	10 bronze coins
pitiful	1 groat

So `lancelot` earns a pitiful yearly salary of only 1 groat — he has his eyes on `guinevere` who clearly possesses more than just good looks. In section 10.8 the plot thickens but in the meanwhile it is necessary to define the application protocol used by the QUERY class clients to communicate with the DATABASE class server. The QUERY objects can send one of two types of command (write or read) to the DATABASE object which in each case can send back one of two types of response (positive or negative acknowledgement). The format of the write command is as follows:

'W'	name	'0'	number	'0'

The first character (`'W'`) indicates a write command and this is followed by two NULL terminated strings — the first string specifies the name to place in the database key column whilst the second gives the corresponding telephone number. This format permits use of variable length commands to improve the efficiency of the network communications — however, for the sake of simplicity the QUERY and DATABASE classes actually use a fixed length message for both commands and responses. If the server is able to obey a write command by adding the new entry to the table then it returns a positive acknowledgement — otherwise a negative acknowledgement is returned in response. The formats of the responses to the write command are as follows:

positive acknowledgement	negative acknowledgement
'Y'	'N'

The read command contains the name of the person for whom a telephone number is required — the format comprises an initial character (`'R'`) to specify a read command followed by a NULL terminated string:

'R'	name	'0'

A similar format is used for a positive acknowledgement to the read command since this includes the requested number stored as a string — the corresponding negative acknowledgement just contains the initial `'N'` character code:

<table>
<tr><td align="center">positive
acknowledgement</td><td align="center">negative
acknowledgement</td></tr>
<tr><td>

`'Y'`	number	`'0'`

</td><td>

`'N'`

</td></tr>
</table>

The following two sections illustrate in detail how these command and response messages are constructed by the sender, transmitted across the network and finally decoded by the receiver.

10.6 The QUERY Class

The QUERY class creates objects that can send commands to the database server and correctly interpret the responses — the QUERY class Run() function is basically a loop that firstly asks the user for a command, then communicates with the server using the protocol defined in the previous section and finally prints out the result. The full specification for the QUERY class is as follows:

```
class QUERY {
public:
   QUERY(void);
   ~QUERY(void);
   void Run(void);
private:
   char GetOption(void);
   void SetupWrite(char*);
   void SetupRead(char*);
};
```

The QUERY class Run() function defines the general operation of a QUERY object — the helper functions GetOption(), SetupWrite() and SetupRead() are invoked to perform specific operations. The Run() function starts by creating a STREAM object with which to talk to the database server — as explained in section 10.4 the construction process will block until a connection is established. The Run() function then enters a loop which (as noted at the start of the section) performs some fairly straightforward processing:

1. The GetOption() function prompts the user for a command

2. Either SetupWrite() or SetupRead() sets up the command message ready for transmission to the server

3. The STREAM object sends the command to the server and then waits to receive the response back

4. The result is displayed for the user

Generally speaking, once the Run() function has finished processing one command it loops back to process the next — the loop is only ever exited when the user decides to quit or else some sort of error occurs.

```cpp
void QUERY::Run(void) {
  STREAM stream(DATABASE_HOST,DATABASE_PORT);
  char command[DATABASE_MESSAGE_SIZE];
  char response[DATABASE_MESSAGE_SIZE];
  int length = DATABASE_MESSAGE_SIZE;
  int done = FALSE;
  char option;
  while (!done) {
    option = GetOption();
    switch (option) {
    case 'W':
      SetupWrite(command);
      if ((stream.Write(command,length)!=-1) &&
          (stream.Read(response,length)!=-1))
        printf("Database Updated\n");
      else
        done = TRUE;
      break;
    case 'R':
      SetupRead(command);
      if ((stream.Write(command,length)!=-1) &&
          (stream.Read(response,length)!=-1))
        switch (response[0]) {
        case 'Y':
          printf("Number is [%s]\n",&response[1]);
          break;
        case 'N':
          printf("Number is Unknown\n");
          break;
        }
      else
        done = TRUE;
      break;
    case 'Q':
      done = TRUE;
      break;
    }
  }
  printf("Exiting ...\n");
}
```

As mentioned in the previous section the application protocol between the QUERY and DATABASE objects uses fixed size messages of length DATABASE_MESSAGE_SIZE — this is somewhat wasteful of network capacity but it does keep the design simple. The QUERY class GetOption() function just prints out a menu and waits for the user to select an option:

```
char QUERY::GetOption(void) {
  char buffer[100];
  printf("Select Option:\n");
  printf("(W) Write To Database\n");
  printf("(R) Read From Database\n");
  printf("(Q) Quit\n");
  scanf("%s\n",buffer);
  return buffer[0];
}
```

The QUERY class SetupWrite() function asks for the name and number to be entered into the database and places these into a buffer that holds the write command message:

```
void QUERY::SetupWrite(char* command) {
  command[0] = 'W';
  printf("Enter Name:\n");
  scanf("%s\n",++command);
  command += strlen(command);
  printf("Enter Number:\n");
  scanf("%s\n",++command);
}
```

Similarly the QUERY class SetupRead() function requests the name of the person whose number is required and then packs this into a buffer to set up the read command message:

```
void QUERY::SetupRead(char* command) {
  command[0] = 'R';
  printf("Enter Name:\n");
  scanf("%s\n",++command);
}
```

The QUERY class is now complete — it is entirely single-threaded and so multiple processes are required to create several clients for the database server. By contrast the DATABASE class described in the following section is most definitely multi-threaded — since the DATABASE object must simultaneously interact with a whole host of QUERY objects it makes good sense to split the object's internal processing into separate tasks and assign a different thread to each one.

10.7 The DATABASE Class

The DATABASE class defines the LISTENER, TALKER and WORKER nested classes to assist in implementing the functionality of a DATABASE object. Each DATABASE object uses one LISTENER object to listen for incoming connection requests from QUERY class clients — the LISTENER object listens at a 'well-known port' defined by the constant DATABASE_PORT so that the clients know how to contact the server. Once a connection between client and server has been established, the LISTENER object passes on the responsibility for further communication with the QUERY object to a TALKER object — there are several TALKER objects within a DATABASE object and each one talks only to its assigned QUERY object. Finally, the WORKER class is designed to actually manipulate the database — again each DATABASE object has several WORKER objects so that multiple database queries are possible at the same time. The following figure illustrates the interconnection of the various bits and pieces within a DATABASE object:

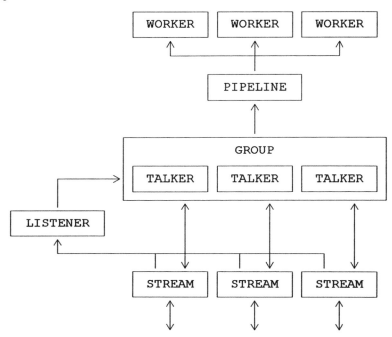

The LISTENER object creates a new STREAM object each time it starts to listen for another client. As soon as the stream is connected the LISTENER object assigns it to one of the TALKER objects by calling its Assign() function — the LISTENER object obtains the TALKER object from a custom resource pool whose GROUP class is derived from the base POOL class described in section 5.4. The TALKER object has previously registered itself with the GROUP object as being free — all of the TALKER objects are initially free, they become busy whilst dealing with the sequence of commands from one particular client and then they return to being free whenever the client disconnects and the associated STREAM object is destroyed. Each TALKER object receives commands and sends back responses via the STREAM object which it is assigned — the STREAM object communicates across the network with the corresponding STREAM object in a QUERY client. Whenever a TALKER object receives a command from its QUERY object it passes the request on to the set of WORKER objects using a PIPELINE object — the messages sent through the pipeline could each contain all the information required to carry out a particular command but instead the TALKER object just passes a pointer to itself. At the far end of the pipeline the various requests are pulled off one at a time as the individual WORKER objects become free. A WORKER object uses the TALKER* pointer in each pipeline message to bind to the appropriate TALKER object by calling its Bind() function, then the WORKER object processes the command and finally it signals to the TALKER object that the response is ready by calling its Unbind() function. The WORKER object binds to the TALKER object so that it can share its Command and Response buffers — this technique avoids some unnecessary copying of data between TALKER and WORKER objects thus improving efficiency. The full specification for the DATABASE class is as follows:

```
class DATABASE {
  class LISTENER {
      ...
  };
  class TALKER : public THREAD {
      ...
  };
  class WORKER : public THREAD {
      ...
  };
  class GROUP : public POOL {
      ...
  };
friend class LISTENER;
friend class TALKER;
friend class WORKER;
public:
  DATABASE(void);
  ~DATABASE(void);
  void Run(void);
private:
  LISTENER* Listener;
  WORKER* Workers[DATABASE_WORKERS];
  ARBITRATOR* Arbitrator;
  PIPELINE Pipeline;
  GROUP* Group;
  ITEM* Head;
  int Count;
};
```

The DATABASE class specification contains the specifications for the nested classes LISTENER, TALKER and WORKER — there is also a nested GROUP class which derives from the base POOL class described in section 5.4. The only other

point of interest is that the database is implemented as a linked list using the Head
and Count fields — the ARBITRATOR object is needed to protect this data
structure when it is being manipulated by multiple WORKER objects. The
DATABASE class also has a number of associated constants:

```
const char* const DATABASE_HOST = "arthur";
const int DATABASE_PORT = 5000;
const int DATABASE_WORKERS = 3;
const int DATABASE_TALKERS = 3;
const int DATABASE_MESSAGE_SIZE = 100;
```

The DATABASE class constructor simply creates all the internal objects needed by
the DATABASE object:

```
DATABASE::DATABASE(void) {
  for (int i=0; (i<DATABASE_WORKERS); i++)
    Workers[i] = new WORKER(this);
  Arbitrator = new ARBITRATOR(DATABASE_WORKERS);
  Listener = new LISTENER(this);
  Group = new GROUP(this);
  Head = new ITEM(NULL);
  Count = 0;
}
```

The WORKER, LISTENER and GROUP class constructors all receive pointers to the
DATABASE object — the GROUP object will pass this pointer along to the TALKER
objects whenever it creates them. The DATABASE class makes the LISTENER,
TALKER and WORKER classes all into friend classes of the DATABASE class so that
the DATABASE* pointer held by objects of these classes can be used to freely
manipulate the private fields of the containing DATABASE object. The DATABASE
class Run() function is responsible for starting up all the internal threads:

```
void DATABASE::Run(void) {
  for (int i=0; (i<DATABASE_WORKERS); i++)
    Workers[i]->Start();
  Group->Activate();
  Listener->Run();
}
```

The GROUP class Activate() function just calls the Start() function for each
of the TALKER objects — both the TALKER and WORKER classes inherit their
Start() function from the THREAD base class and this function starts up a new
thread when it is invoked. Conversely, the LISTENER class Run() function does
not start another thread but instead enters an endless loop listening for connection
requests from QUERY objects. Ideally the DATABASE class destructor should break
the LISTENER object out of its loop, stop all the internal threads and then perform
any cleanup which is necessary — however, for simplicity the approach taken here

is to note that the DATABASE class Run() function will never return and consequently to assume that the DATABASE object will not be destroyed. The DATABASE class destructor therefore does nothing:

```
DATABASE::~DATABASE(void) {}
```

The full specification for the nested LISTENER class is as follows:

```
class LISTENER {
public:
  LISTENER(DATABASE*);
  ~LISTENER(void);
  void Run(void);
private:
  DATABASE* Database;
};
```

The LISTENER class constructor simply stores the back-pointer to the enclosing DATABASE object in its Database field whilst the LISTENER class destructor does nothing:

```
DATABASE::LISTENER::LISTENER(DATABASE* database) {
  Database = database;
}
```

```
DATABASE::LISTENER::~LISTENER(void) {}
```

The LISTENER class Run() function loops endlessly listening for connection requests from QUERY object clients:

```
void DATABASE::LISTENER::Run(void) {
  TALKER* talker;
  STREAM* stream;
  while (TRUE) {
    talker = (TALKER*)(Database->Group->Allocate());
    stream = new STREAM((char*)NULL,DATABASE_PORT);
    talker->Assign(stream);
  }
}
```

The loop firstly requests a free TALKER object from the resource pool and waits in the GROUP class Allocate() function until one is available. Next a new STREAM object is created with completion of the construction process being delayed until a connection is made. Finally, the LISTENER object assigns the further handling of the stream to the TALKER object and then loops back to process the next incoming connection.

The nested GROUP class has the following specification:

```
class GROUP : public POOL {
public:
  GROUP(DATABASE*);
  ~GROUP(void);
  void Activate(void);
};
```

As discussed in section 5.4 the GROUP class constructor is responsible for filling the Resources array with the resources specific to that derived class but the base class destructor takes care of destroying these resources so that the derived class destructor need perform no processing:

```
DATABASE::GROUP::GROUP(DATABASE* database)
        : POOL(DATABASE_TALKERS) {
  for (int i=0; (i<DATABASE_TALKERS); i++)
    Resources[i] = new TALKER(database);
}

DATABASE::GROUP::~GROUP(void) {}
```

The GROUP class Activate() function loops through the array of TALKER object resources and calls Start() for each one to start its internal thread:

```
void DATABASE::GROUP::Activate(void) {
  for (int i=0; (i<DATABASE_TALKERS); i++)
    ((TALKER*)Resources[i])->Start();
}
```

The specification for the nested TALKER class is as follows:

```
class TALKER : public THREAD {
public:
  TALKER(DATABASE*);
  ~TALKER(void);
  void Assign(STREAM*);
  void Bind(char**,char**);
  void Unbind(void);
protected:
  virtual void* Run(void*);
private:
  DATABASE* Database;
  STREAM* Stream;
  EVENT Go;
  EVENT Ready;
  char Command[DATABASE_MESSAGE_SIZE];
  char Response[DATABASE_MESSAGE_SIZE];
};
```

The TALKER class is probably the most complicated element of the distributed database design since it must interact with practically everything else. Like the LISTENER class, the TALKER class constructor just stores a back-pointer to the DATABASE object in its Database field — the TALKER object receives its DATABASE* pointer from the GROUP class constructor.

```
DATABASE::TALKER::TALKER(DATABASE* database) {
  Database = database;
}
```

The TALKER class destructor performs no processing:

```
DATABASE::TALKER::~TALKER(void) {}
```

The TALKER class Run() function coordinates most of the activities occurring within the DATABASE object:

```
void* DATABASE::TALKER::Run(void*) {
  int length = DATABASE_MESSAGE_SIZE;
  while (TRUE) {
    Go.Wait();
    while (Stream->Read(Command,length) != -1) {
      Database->Pipeline.Put(this);
      Ready.Wait();
      if (Stream->Write(Response,length) == -1)
        break;
    }
    Stream->Close();
    delete Stream;
    Database->Group->Deallocate(this);
  }
  return NULL;
}
```

Within its endless **while** loop, the TALKER class Run() function firstly waits on the Go event for a signal from the LISTENER object that there is a stream connected to a QUERY object for the TALKER object to manage — the LISTENER object sets the TALKER object's Stream field and signals its Go event by calling the TALKER class Assign() function:

```
void DATABASE::TALKER::Assign(STREAM* stream) {
  Stream = stream;
  Go.Signal();
}
```

Next the TALKER class Run() function enters an inner loop that processes the sequence of command messages received from the stream. Each message is read into the Command buffer and then the TALKER object passes its **this** pointer through the pipeline to act as a 'work request' for the WORKER objects — the

TALKER object subsequently waits on the Ready event. As soon as one of the WORKER objects becomes free it pulls the first work request from the head of the pipeline — eventually one of the WORKER objects will respond to the request just posted. The WORKER object then binds with the TALKER object by calling its Bind() function — this enables the WORKER object to use the TALKER object's Command and Response buffers directly:

```
void DATABASE::TALKER::Bind(char** command,
                            char** response) {
  *command = Command;
  *response = Response;
}
```

Next the WORKER object manipulates the database entries to carry out the command specified in the Command buffer and eventually it returns the corresponding response in the Response buffer — when the WORKER object has finished it calls the TALKER class Unbind() function to reawaken the TALKER object:

```
void DATABASE::TALKER::Unbind(void) {
  Ready.Signal();
}
```

The TALKER object then sends the response back through the stream to the QUERY object and loops to receive the next command. Eventually the stream will disconnect — this is almost certainly a sign that the user has instructed the QUERY object client to quit but there may also be network problems. In any case the TALKER object exits its inner loop and then closes the stream and deletes the STREAM object. Finally, the TALKER object calls the GROUP class Deallocate() function to register itself as being free again. The last piece in the DATABASE class puzzle is the nested WORKER class — this class has the following specification:

```
class WORKER : public THREAD {
public:
  WORKER(DATABASE*);
  ~WORKER(void);
protected:
  virtual void* Run(void*);
private:
  void WriteDatabase(char*,char*);
  void ReadDatabase(char*,char*);
  DATABASE* Database;
};
```

As with the `LISTENER` and `TALKER` classes the `WORKER` class constructor just stores the back-pointer to the containing `DATABASE` object and the `WORKER` class destructor does nothing:

```
DATABASE::WORKER::WORKER(DATABASE* database) {
  Database = database;
}

DATABASE::WORKER::~WORKER(void) {}
```

The `WORKER` class `Run()` function is executed by an internal thread and processes the work requests sent through the pipeline by the `TALKER` objects:

```
void* DATABASE::WORKER::Run(void*) {
  TALKER* talker;
  char* command;
  char* response;
  while (TRUE) {
    talker = (TALKER*)(Database->Pipeline.Get());
    talker->Bind(&command,&response);
    switch (command[0]) {
    case 'W':
      Database->Arbitrator->WriterLock();
      WriteDatabase(command,response);
      Database->Arbitrator->WriterUnlock();
      break;
    case 'R':
      Database->Arbitrator->ReaderLock();
      ReadDatabase(command,response);
      Database->Arbitrator->ReaderUnlock();
      break;
    }
    talker->Unbind();
  }
  return NULL;
}
```

Within the endless loop, the `WORKER` class `Run()` function starts by pulling the first `TALKER*` pointer from the pipeline and binding to the corresponding `TALKER` object. The `WORKER` object then decodes the command held by the `TALKER` object and calls either `WriteDatabase()` or `ReadDatabase()` according to whether a write or read command has been received — these functions update the `TALKER` object's response buffer appropriately. In both cases the `Arbitrator` object is used to ensure the integrity of the database — for a write command the `WriteDatabase()` call is preceded by a call to `WriterLock()`

and followed by a call to `WriterUnlock()` whilst for a read command the `ReadDatabase()` function is similarly sandwiched between `ReaderLock()` and `ReaderUnlock()` functions. Once the command has been processed, the WORKER object signals to the TALKER object by calling its `Unbind()` function and then it loops back round to handle the next work request from the pipeline. As previously noted the database is implemented using a linked list with the DATABASE class `Head` field pointing to the head ITEM object in the list — section 5.5 covers the ITEM class and in particular it explains how the `Head` item is actually a dummy item present only to simplify the processing of the list. Each of the remaining items in the list contain a pointer to an ENTRY structure — this structure has `Key` and `Value` fields which are used here to reference 'name' and 'number' elements of each database entry:

```
struct ENTRY {
  char* Key;
  char* Value;
};
```

The WORKER class `WriteDatabase()` and `ReadDatabase()` functions are responsible for actually maintaining the database — the `WriteDatabase()` function has the following definition:

```
void DATABASE::WORKER::WriteDatabase(char* command,
                                     char* response) {
  ENTRY* entry = new ENTRY;
  int length = strlen(++command);
  entry->Key = new char[++length];
  memcpy(entry->Key,command,length);
  command += length;
  length = strlen(command);
  entry->Value = new char[++length];
  memcpy(entry->Value,command,length);
  ITEM* item = new ITEM(entry);
  item->Append(Database->Head);
  Database->Count++;
  response[0] = 'Y';
}
```

The `WriteDatabase()` function creates a new ENTRY structure and also allocates new storage for the `Key` and `Value` strings — the name and number information is then copied from the write command message before the ENTRY structure is wrapped by an ITEM object and added to the database list. Finally, the count of list items is incremented and the response message is constructed — the simple implementation presented here assumes that the write command will always succeed.

The WORKER class ReadDatabase() function is defined as follows:

```
void DATABASE::WORKER::ReadDatabase(char* command,
                                    char* response) {
  ITEM* item = Database->Head;
  ENTRY* entry;
  int i;
  command++;
  for (i=0; (i<Database->Count); i++) {
    item = item->GetNext();
    entry = (ENTRY*)item->GetData();
    if (strcmp(entry->Key,command) == 0)
      break;
  }
  if (i < Database->Count) {
    response[0] = 'Y';
    strcpy(++response,entry->Value);
  }
  else
    response[0] = 'N';
}
```

First the ReadDatabase() function scans through the list of ITEM objects comparing the name specified in the read command with the Key string of each ENTRY object. If a match is found then the corresponding Value string is copied into the 'number' field of a positive response message — otherwise a negative response message is created.

10.8 Building the Application

To demonstrate the full power of the distributed database application, the server process and each of the client processes should be run on a separate computer — however, if this is impractical it is also possible for all these processes to be run on a single machine with each process automatically binding to a different port. In any case the name of the server machine is specified by the DATABASE_HOST string constant:

```
const char* const DATABASE_HOST = "arthur";
```

On this host the database process must execute the following trivial piece of code:

```
int main(int argc, char** argv) {
  DATABASE database;
  database.Run();
  return 0;
}
```

The main() function for the query process on a client machine is equally
straightforward:

```
int main(int argc, char** argv) {
  QUERY query;
  query.Run();
  return 0;
}
```

Now, continuing the example from section 10.5, suppose that in addition to the
arthur server there are also guinevere, lancelot and merlin clients.
Immediately after startup each of the clients uses a write command to add their
telephone number to the database — the following figure depicts the resultant
database table:

name	number
guinevere	123
lancelot	456
merlin	789

Now lancelot lusting after guinevere and her substantial income asks
arthur for her number — the output of the lancelot client appears as follows:

```
Select Option:
(W) Write To Database
(R) Read From Database
(Q) Quit
W
Enter Name:
lancelot
Enter Number:
456
Database Updated
Select Option:
(W) Write To Database
(R) Read From Database
(Q) Quit
R
Enter Name:
guinevere
Number is [123]
Select Option:
(W) Write To Database
(R) Read From Database
(Q) Quit
Q
Exiting ...
```

With this important piece of information finally in his possession, lancelot suddenly remembers that his telephone was disconnected when he failed to pay the bill so he rushes off to the nearest pay-phone to invest this year's groat on an important call.

10.9 Summary

This chapter has described the implementation of a distributed database application with the main objective being to provide an extended example of multi-threaded programming in C++ that combines the building blocks from earlier chapters into something approaching the complexity of real-world code. The application comprises a database server based on the DATABASE class along with a collection of clients that are constructed using the QUERY class — the clients are actually single-threaded but the server, which must interact with several different clients simultaneously, is most naturally implemented in a multi-threaded manner. The database server is intended to be run on one computer whilst each of the clients execute on other machines connected to the first by means of a network — the communications between the server and its clients is achieved using the STREAM class which permits a stream of bytes to be transmitted reliably between sender and receiver. The STREAM class exists basically to implement the functionality specified by the STREAM_INTERFACE class and it is in fact just a wrapper for the CHANNEL class that actually encapsulates the services provided by the connection-oriented TCP network protocol — the TCP/IP suite of communications protocols was originally introduced by the fledgling Internet and is concerned with such things as hosts, ports and sockets. The DATABASE class itself is really quite simple since the various tasks associated with managing the database are delegated to the nested LISTENER, TALKER and WORKER classes — a LISTENER object listens for incoming connection requests from QUERY class clients, several TALKER objects manage the network communications with the clients as they issue write and read commands, and a set of WORKER objects process these commands and actually manipulate the information held by the database. The DATABASE class along with its nested helper classes implement a rudimentary form of relational database management system (RDBMS) — a relational database comprises a set of cross-referenced tables with each table containing a collection of 'key-value' entries. The QUERY and DATABASE classes together provide the basic elements for a realistic distributed database application — this foundation could easily be extended to create a more useful product.

Postscript

This book has hopefully provided you, the reader, with a practical introduction to multi-threaded programming in C++. The journey has been a long one but many useful C++ classes should now be familiar friends:

— the fundamental THREAD class
— synchronization primitive classes MUTEX and EVENT
— the versatile SYNCH synchronization class
— the utility SEMAPHORE class
— more specialized classes RECURSIVE_MUTEX and MULTI_EVENT
— the POOL and ARBITRATOR classes for resource management
— the KEY class for thread-specific storage
— the ONCE class for one-time initialization
— the ATOMIC class for atomic operations
— the TIMER class for scheduling future activities
— standardized communications classes TRANSFER and STREAM
— inter-thread buffering classes PIPELINE and BUFFER
— the CHANNEL class for network connections
— the MUX and DEMUX classes for message multiplexing

But the real adventure is just beginning — now that you're properly equipped to face the challenge, a bright new world of multi-threaded applications awaits you ...

Index

U

W